DECORATING IN DETAIL

ALEXA HAMPTON

DECORATING IN DETAIL

WITH JILL KIRCHNER SIMPSON
PHOTOGRAPHS BY STEVE FREIHON

POTTER STYLE
NEW YORK

For Lana Lawrence,
A beloved friend, a trusted colleague,
and a true inspiration

And, of course, for Pavlos,
Michalis, Markos, and Aliki

Published in the United States by Potter Style, an imprint of the Crown Publishing Group,
a division of Random House, Inc., New York.
www.crownpublishing.com
www.clarksonpotter.com

Potter Style is a trademark and POTTER with colophon is
a registered trademark of Random House, Inc.

Library of Congress Cataloging-in-Publication Data
Hampton, Alexa.
  Decorating in detail / Alexa Hampton. —First Edition.
     pages cm
 1. Hampton, Alexa—Themes, motives. 2. Interior decoration—United States. I. Title.
 NK2004.3.H36A4 2013
 747.0973—dc23   2012049502

ISBN 978-0-307-95685-9

Printed in China

All photos by Steve Freihon, with exception of photos on pages 11, 12, 14, 16, 19–18, 20, 21,
24–25, 26–27, 30, 32, 33, 34–35, 37, 40, and 41 copyright © 2013 by Scott Frances; and on pages
45, 47, 48–49, 50, 52–53, 58, 60–61, and 64–65 copyright © 2013 by Durston Saylor

Book and jacket design by Doug Turshen with Steve Turner
Jacket photographs © Steve Freihon
10 9 8 7 6 5 4 3 2 1
First Edition

CONTENTS

INTRODUCTION

I grew up in the 1980s. I worked summers in my father's office through the better part of that go-go decade, when the mantra was "More" and no detail was left untouched—everything was gilded, fringed, polished, and layered to within an inch of its life. So I understood when the tidal wave reaction came: People started worshipping at the temple of minimalism, "neutral" became a color, and "midcentury modern" became Mecca. I had my own rebellion to years of growing up awash in Colefax and Fowler prints and brush fringe. For several years after my father died, I didn't much care for trim. I could see why everyone felt the need to molt all that detritus. So I did away with much of it (and I stopped wearing skirts to work, too!).

However, I've come back around over time. In an age when everyone can buy the same sofa silhouette, whether it's from George Smith or Crate & Barrel, and find all the same fabrics via the Internet, we may have reached the point where the only things that distinguishes us, and our houses, are the details. If we're all going to wear black pants (as I do nearly every day), it requires that we add a few special flourishes of our own. Today, uniqueness has become the ultimate luxury. Details allow you to customize a piece of furniture or curtains to make them yours alone—a one-of-a-kind piece. It doesn't have to mean untold expense or a room overwrought with perfect, stage-directed "moments."

In the best-case scenario, the details and objects you choose have meaning for you—the Fortuny fabric brought back from a trip to Venice, the painting that was a gift from an artist friend, the heirloom china that belonged to your great-grandmother. But even if they are not personal, at least make your choices thoughtful ones: a spaced nailhead on a tape trim; a gray silk lining in a lampshade; a rug that's custom-colored to work perfectly in your room. Bespoke details often require more time, but decorator that I am, I like to think that the result is worth it.

Of course, comfort and function are still paramount. I don't believe in detail for detail's sake; even the smallest elements should always serve a larger whole. In my first book, *The Language of Interior Design*, I laid out the four elements that form the structure of a successful room—contrast, proportion, color, and balance. In this book, I want to drill down to the next level, to zoom in, from macro to micro, on the details that help complete a room. It is the finishing touches that make a house feel polished, and help it function smoothly. Just as essential as finding suitable fabrics and

trims is enlisting the right technology so that you can watch TV in bed comfortably, or charge your phone with ease, or dim the lights and draw the blinds at the touch of a well-placed button.

It's also in these details and customization that a designer can truly make a difference, as he or she can offer options and resources to create a room that's like no other, one that suits you to a *T* because you bothered to dot the *i*'s. When details are done right, they don't stand out; they draw you in: the closer you look, the more there is to appreciate and enjoy.

The houses and apartments in this book are projects my firm and I worked on from start to finish. Each in its own way helps demonstrate how attention to detail can make an amazing difference. Interspersed throughout, and also in depth at the back of the book, I offer some key guidelines, from how high to hang curtains, artwork, chair rails, and sconces to what type of curtain rod or door pull to use, to the pros and cons of various styles of upholstery. I hope this book will inspire and empower you to look at your own house with a fresh eye and with attention to every detail.

PREVIOUS PAGES: In a bedroom in a modern high-rise, we transformed a featureless box with elegant silk curtains, lacquered charcoal walls, a luminous silver-leaf ceiling, and a stunning chinoiserie screen. ABOVE: If John Soane lived in a contemporary apartment, this is what I envisioned his dressing room might look like. On a severe time constraint, we painted the paneling to look like mahogany, bound fabric as rugs, and upholstered the walls in a crisp tailored stripe.

HOT AND COLD

Located in a gracious 1930 building on Central Park, this spacious apartment hadn't been touched since 1969—not a banner year for design, in my estimation. While that history might sound off-putting, to me it meant that much of the architectural detail and graceful flow of the original design hadn't been lost through ill-considered renovations over the years. Yet we certainly had our work cut out for us: We had to completely renovate all the baths and the kitchen and lay down new wood floors. (The existing floors were concrete with carpet glued on top, an approach I do not endorse.) We decided to restore the old moldings in some places and design new ones in others, and add

millwork throughout the interiors. But this process also allowed us to create exactly the refined pied-à-terre these homeowners envisioned for entertaining their family and friends. This project is probably the only time a client said, "I'm the type of person who makes up my mind and doesn't ask for any change orders," and then kept that promise—there may have been one change order on this entire job, which is truly miraculous.

A few other architectural changes were made to update the layout: Originally this apartment had one very long hallway running the length of the space, creating an uninviting bowling alley effect. The longer and narrower a hallway is, the more claustrophobic it feels. We broke up the hall by creating a vestibule in the center and enlarging the doorways leading into it. This visual pause offers a bit of breathing room.

PREVIOUS PAGES: The bold colors of paintings by Fernand Léger add spark to the quiet grays of the living room. ABOVE: The vestibule beyond the entrance was added to break up a narrow hallway running the length of the apartment. OPPOSITE: The curvaceous swoop of this bench in the entrance hall contrasts with the very rectilinear black-and-white works of art above it.

When a room is swathed in neutrals, adding artwork,
flowers, or a few boldly colored accents
is all it takes to ignite a restrained background.

Installing a low dado or wainscoting in the living room, entrance hall, and hallway vestibule helped emphasize the height of the ceilings and enrich the architectural detail. The marble floor of the entrance hall was changed to wood, to allow for an uninterrupted flow from room to room and to make the entry feel less like an isolated airlock and more like an integral part of the residence. And because the bedroom wing is directly off the entrance hall, swapping in wood dampened the clatter of heels clicking, which the hard marble amplified.

The owner wanted a palette of cool grays for the living room, an idea that greatly appealed to me, but I was concerned about the room feeling too cold if it were simply a monochromatic study in gray. We added *rouge de fer* ("iron red") elements as punctuation marks throughout the room, weaving a thread of fiery warmth through the cool embers of charcoal. Flanking the window, a gorgeous pair of antique chinoiserie screens set the tone in a rich lacquered cinnabar red with the shimmering glow of gilded figures. The screens weren't quite tall enough to create the proper proportion in the room—I didn't want them to bisect the space—so we had 16-inch-high stands built to elevate them.

The Chinese reds are carried through in the lacquered coffee table, the small pouf by the fireplace, and some Fortuny pillows and cashmere throws on the sofas. Splashes of red also figure prominently in the exquisite works of art collected by the owners, including paintings by Léger and Miró. In addition, the honeyed tones of the quarter-sawn oak herringbone floors we chose, and the leafy green interior trees, which visually connect the room with the park outside the windows, bring natural warmth and life to the space.

A cool palette like this (in comparison with the regal reds, golds, and deep greens we typically associate with richly appointed traditional rooms) has a youthful modernity that subverts expectations. The subtlety of the color scheme allowed us to indulge in more ornate trims and

OPPOSITE: The clockface on the fireplace mantel is a piece I used in a show house in 1999, and it serendipitously resurfaced in an antiques store while we were shopping for this apartment. FOLLOWING PAGES: The cinnabar red of the Chinese screens in the corners pops up again in a lacquered cocktail table, round pouf, lamps, and pillows.

ABOVE: French neoclassical furniture juxtaposes with modern art such as this Cubist painting over the bar cabinet, which creates energetic contrasts in a traditional room. OPPOSITE: These beautifully gilded and lacquered Chinese screens were not quite tall enough to form a dramatic backdrop, so we had 16-inch-high wooden stands built to elevate them.

A cool room needs warm accents—such as gold and bronze hardware, picture frames, and other details; and the honeyed warmth of rich woods in floors and furniture.

dressmaker details without it feeling too stuffy, immutable, and old-fashioned. And when you're going to the effort and expense of having custom upholstery made, why not take advantage of the opportunity to make it completely one-of-a-kind?

The thread of red is first introduced in the entrance hall, by way of a distinctive geometric dhurrie rug and chair cushions that give a preview of what's to come. In a similar way, the living room serves as an overture to the adjacent dining room/library, where muted rust reds predominate, taking their cue from the collection of rouge de fer porcelain in the bookcases.

Even in a rather grand New York apartment, space is always at a premium, so it makes sense for the dining room to play multiple roles, rather than sitting empty much of the time. Here it became a library, with the addition of classically detailed cerused-oak bookcases and paneling encasing the room, adding to its warmth. It also serves as a TV room, with the dining table positioned at one end and a comfortable seating arrangement populating the other half. A rouge woven damask on the dining chairs and heathered russet wool curtains continue the terra-cotta tones across the room. The beautifully articulated symmetry of the bookcases brings order to the space and serves another useful purpose: It elegantly camouflages the cluster of three doors that lead to the kitchen, the entry hall, and a closet containing the AV equipment.

The kitchen makes similarly economical use of space. Because this apartment is a pied-à-terre (used for visits, not year-round), the galley kitchen is compact and simple. Its sleek clarity belies the fact that it was actually a complex puzzle to lay out all the pieces of Calacatta marble for the floors, counters, and backsplash so that the veining would feel subtle and uniform. The kitchen floor, like the master bath, features slabs of marble that have been expertly book-matched so that

OPPOSITE: What appears from afar to be a rather monochromatic palette is richly varied upon closer inspection: Multitone gray cording outlines the upholstery, including this damask sofa, enhancing its graphic qualities. Woven pillows with brushed fringe layer in additional texture. The eagle's-head legs and circular motifs on the neoclassical side table introduce the warm, subtle gleam of gold. FOLLOWING PAGES: The hints of terra-cotta red in the living room become more pronounced in the dining room/library. Similar rugs also link the two rooms.

The reds of the living room mellow into russet tones in the dining area. Even in a somewhat formal room, I like the texture and warmth (and light control) that bamboo shades provide.

RICH IN TEXTURE

Upon closer inspection, the monochromatic palettes reveal layers of texture and pattern. **1.** Among the many shades of gray in the living room are the beautiful damask on sofa and chair (right), "Palma" from Claremont; a chairback in a silk/linen stripe, "Belle Aire" from Travers; and pillows in "Chardin Chenille" (top) from Claremont. **2.** The wool dhurrie rug in the entry hall is "Langham Lattice" from Todd Romano. **3.** In the blue guest room, a soft printed silk on curtains, "Soleil Silk Wrap" from Brunschwig & Fils, sets the palette. A wool herringbone from Holland & Sherry (right) upholsters the bed, and the same company's "Palpana Celeste," a woven wool, is on the benches. **4.** In the yellow guest room, an elegant embroidered silk, "Paris" (left) from Cowtan & Tout, used on the square pillows, elevates the entire room. A printed linen, "Camellia" from Hodsoll McKenzie, is its less dressy cousin on curtains. The diamond geometric hand-tufted rug from Beauvais appears in different custom colors in each bedroom. **5.** Elizabeth Eakins's "Linds" damask gains added dimension when tufted on the master bedroom's headboard. Pleats emphasize the vertical axis in the silk check from Christopher Norman seen on curtains. They are trimmed in Clarence House "Tsarina" silk tassel fringe. A silk velvet *gaufrage* (where the pattern is heat-embossed into the fabric), "Liberty" (right) from Christopher Hyland, was used on a bolster pillow and chair. **6.** Pierre Frey's "Thile" woven damask covers the dining chairs. Cowtan & Tout's "Oxford" silk stripe and a woven chenille from Old World Weavers vary the textures on pillows in the dining room/library.

In the galley kitchens so common in urban apartments, the goal is simplicity and uniformity of materials, unlike in their larger suburban cousins.

the veining lines up in a precise mirror image. Using the same material throughout, along with white cabinets, gives the small space a streamlined, open feeling.

Each of the three bedrooms was infused with soft color: shades of sage green in the master bedroom, sky blues in one guest/family bedroom, and golden yellows in another. The owners wanted to maintain a sense of uniformity across the bedrooms, so we used the same curtain treatment with a pretty box-pleated valance in each room, but varied the fabrics; the same diamond-textured wall-to-wall carpet appears in each room, but in different colors. The goal was for the bedrooms to feel like rooms in a luxurious hotel, in the best sense: well-appointed and pampering.

This apartment is at the perfect height for beautiful views: high enough to be filled with light and sky, and low enough to gaze out at the treetops. Muted shades of green in the master bedroom subtly echo this verdant view. Upholstering the walls in a textured silk/cotton and covering the floor in wall-to-wall carpet muffles noise and creates a cocoon of luxurious fabric. I find that upholstered headboards are the most comfortable, both in practice and in their plump visual suggestion of comfort. Here we used a tufted damask on a king-size bed comprised of individual movable beds placed side by side. In monochromatic bedrooms like these, custom-embroidered linens add an essential layer of detail and texture. An interesting footnote: there are twin televisions on a lift concealed within a fabric-covered chest at the foot of the bed. A pivoting TV would have been harder to wire, and with today's flat screens, placing them back-to-back, for viewing from the bed or the seating area, was the preferred solution.

A long, narrow galley kitchen feels more open and airy thanks to creamy white cabinets and lightly veined Calacatta marble that is used uniformly on the floors, counters, and backsplash. Appliances such as the black stove and wine refrigerator provide the only notes of contrast.

In the master bedroom, soothing shades of green connect to the leafy views of Central Park. Upholstered walls, a tufted damask headboard, and wall-to-wall carpeting muffle sound and envelop the space in softness. Elegant neoclassical furniture mixes with modern-day amenities such as back-to-back TVs concealed in a chest at the foot of the bed.

Originally, the blue bedroom was a library off the living room. We ripped it up, closed it off, and gave it an en suite bath and closet. A single upholstered headboard embraces two beds that can be made up as twins or a king, depending on the guests staying here. Dark wood Biedermeier bedside chests and benches at the foot of the bed add an important note of contrast in this becalmed sea of soft blues. I am always a fan of bamboo blinds (and motorized blackout shades) beneath the curtains to provide light control and privacy as well as natural texture.

Sunny hues of yellow bring light to the back bedroom. Two full-size beds allow for the most versatile sleeping options, and shaped upholstered headboards add architectural interest and geometric composition to a long wall. This room includes an important feature we added to the windows throughout the apartment: mirrored reveals, or side panels of the window bays (seen on page 38), which reflect the views down toward the park and increase the amount of light in the room. In this room especially, located at the building's back corner, it was important to see glimpses of greenery among the brickwork of the surrounding buildings. Elegant embroidered pillows and bed linens exhibit the homeowners' unflagging attention to detail, even in the least prominent of rooms.

An all-white marble bath is a classic. It feels clean, light, and bright and will never go out of style. Chrome fixtures and monogrammed white bath linens are equally timeless.

Crema Delicato marble covers nearly every inch of this sumptuous master bath. The marble on the walls and the tub surround is paneled like wood, in a honed finish so it's not slippery. (The shower floor is sanded, and slightly slanted so it drains well.) The veining of the marble is matched across the pilasters, and the bottom panels are book-matched, creating a mirror image of the veining in the panels above. Heated floors keep the marble feeling warm underfoot.

CLOSET CONSIDERATIONS

The wife's closet/dressing room functions as a passageway to the master bathroom, so everything is hidden behind closed doors. It illustrates some of the most important elements to incorporate (or avoid) in closets.

- Hanging space need not be any deeper than 24 inches (the depth of a large coat on a hanger). Given this dimension, we were able to take unneeded space away from her closet and give it to his.

- I like to include a built-in bureau with outlets for a charging station, with side mirrors that pivot so you can check the back of your head. The height of the bureau should be keyed to the height of the user.

- Similarly, the height of hanging rods should also be subtly adjusted to the height of the user. A man with long legs will need a rod for trousers hung higher than will a man of the same height with a long torso. Start with the dimension of the bottom rod and work upward. I recommend placing a fixed shelf above the top rod. Make the top shelf narrower to allow room to easily reach objects.

- In a large closet or dressing room, an island in the center is ideal for packing and folding. You can incorporate drawers on one or several sides, depending on the depth required.

- I tend to prefer flat shelves for shoes, unless the shelves are low and in a compact space; then, tilted shelves allow the shoes to be seen more easily. Flat shelves are more versatile because they can easily be reassigned to pocketbooks, hats, or other items as needed. Slide-out shelves are particularly helpful, but cannot be made adjustable.

- I used to build in hampers, but for ventilation, a mesh hamper or wicker bin (often with a liner) that can be carried to the laundry is preferable.

- Good lighting is essential. In a closed-door closet, you'll want to have jamb switching, which turns the lights on and off automatically when you open and close the door. Instead of overhead lighting, which can be obstructed by large objects on upper shelves, fluorescent tubes located just inside the interior door casing are a smart idea. In walk-in closets, a combination of strip lights and overhead lighting, all on dimmers, is most useful.

- Consider adding locked drawers (or a safe) for jewelry and other valuables.

- Hardware for half-doors and drawers in a walk-in closet should usually be scaled smaller than that of standard-size doors and drawers.

Paneled doors mirrored only on the top half bring in light without overdoing it, so you don't feel bombarded with multiple full-length images. This closet also has the luxury of natural light from windows. Walk-in closets and baths are two of the few places I use overhead light fixtures.

ABOVE: A yellow color scheme helps compensate for less light in this back bedroom. Two full-size beds afforded room to create headboards with shapely profiles. Details such as the embroidered silk pillows, bolsters, and piqué matelassé covers help embellish the room.
OPPOSITE: This room was originally a library off the living room. What was a dark paneled room has become light and soothing bathed in soft blues. The curtains and carpet in each of the three bedrooms are the same style, executed in different fabrics and colors.

DEFINING DETAILS

The silhouettes of furniture—the curve of an arm, the eagle's head on a tripod table, the sensuous scroll of a bench—add an important element of interest to any room. They draw an elegant line not only with their form, but also in the shape of the negative space around them.

1. Key tassels are a wonderful little bit of frippery that actually serves a purpose: You're much less likely to misplace the key! Here, the tassel draws attention to the metal lattice detail on this chest in the living room. **2.** The red lacquered table, hints of russet in the rug, and the warmth of gilded wood furniture contrast with the cool gray upholstery, walls, and curtains. **3.** The neoclassical furniture in the yellow guest room is detailed with gilded fluting, and carved turnings accent the curved arms and legs of the desk chair. **4.** In the library, we custom-built this leather-topped end table because small end tables can be hard to come by. It is purposely lower than the sofa arm so as not to interfere with the view of the sofa's attractive silhouette from the living room. **5.** Even on a simple bedroom chair, there's an opportunity to add a little twinkle of detail, such as these spaced nailheads. **6.** I love arranging bookshelves, and prefer to organize the books by height if possible, for a tidy composition. Hanging artwork from shelves adds variety, as long as the pictures can be moved to access books when needed.

3

Every surface offers an opportunity to create a pleasing composition. Consider how coffee tables look from above, and how dressers appear from the side.

1. We replaced an undistinguished mantel with this ornately detailed marble one. **2.** I love the fact that the Léger monograph on the coffee table corresponds with the artwork on the walls, while also picking up on the red of the lacquer table. I pay particular attention to tabletop arrangements, forming careful compositions with the *objets*. The polished piece of wood is actually an antique Japanese neck pillow. **3.** The bed in the master bedroom mixes a cotton damask–tufted headboard with green silk European squares and a leafy embroidered duvet. The silk velvet *gaufrage* bolster pillow matches the chairs in the room. **4.** The heathered cord-on-tape that outlines the sofa was also used to create a flower-like tasseled frog at the end of each arm. I love these moments of pure ornament, though they no doubt originally served a purpose, such as gathering fabric or camouflaging seams. **5.** The quirky, organic forms of these Cocteau-like coral branches provide a marked contrast with the strict linear form of the neoclassical chest. **6.** An exquisite red Fortuny pillow stands out against a mix of gray patterns and textures on the sofa.

6

THE SHAPE OF
THINGS TO COME

This young family's house in Connecticut is the happy result of a collaboration between architect Joel Barkley, who was inspired by traditional Swedish architecture; homeowners with great taste who knew exactly what they wanted; and my firm. The front exterior—black clapboard with crisp white trim—is striking but not austere. (The other side of the house is white; we call it the "Oreo cookie house" behind its back.) It sounds crazy but it looks amazing.

On any given project, one of the greatest concerns is how to appropriately marry the interiors to the exteriors. I am very sensitive to this question, because I think it is very important to have an explicit relationship between inside and outside. As a New Yorker, I am

The striking black-and-white exterior gives a traditional country house a more modern, graphic edge and serves as a dramatic backdrop for the lush lawn and gardens.

programmed to be more free in my approach to interiors. After all, we city folk all live in cubes floating above the ground that bear little to no relationship to the façades of our buildings. This freedom is quite liberating, but it can create bad habits. In fact, whenever I have looked for an apartment, I have always considered the façade opposite me more important than that of the building which housed the apartment I was thinking of buying—a truly bizarre approach, but that view is what I would see on a daily basis.

The choice with interiors is to go either with or against the exterior design. In this case, we chose to create a contrast. That is not to suggest that the two fight each other. Rather, we made the interiors the natural, equal and opposite reaction to the stark white-and-black façade.

The graphic black-and-white palette cuts the sweetness of the Gustavian blues and lavenders woven throughout the neo-Swedish/American interior. Each room opens onto the next—there are few hallways—so a consistent palette across the rooms made abundant sense. The other constant is an emphasis on shape and silhouette. We had great fun playing with the geometry of ellipses and arabesques, trellis and lattice patterns, quatrefoils and grids. And despite the fact that this is a welcoming home to four young children, there is no sacrifice of style.

The front door leads down a hall to a foyer with a grand fireplace and two quatrefoil chairs. This space, which gives onto the living room, dining room, and staircase, serves as a fulcrum between the two wings of the house. The living room is organized into two areas, with a sofa and upholstered chairs gathered by a fireplace at one end, and a round table and chairs near the French doors at the other. I love center tables like these, which are an inviting spot for playing games,

PREVIOUS PAGE: The foyer serves as the pivot point between the two wings of this Swedish-inspired house. OPPOSITE: The farmhouse-style Dutch door opens onto the back terrace.

doing homework, or enjoying a cozy dinner. Encircling it are the signature loops of Frances Elkins's iconic chairs, which signify that this is a house whose owners not only know and care about design, but also have the confidence to embrace touches of whimsy. The curlicues of the chairs are echoed in the embroidered lavender arabesques of the curtains. And like the exterior of the house, the softness of the palette is contrasted with the black Napoleon III bookcase.

At the seating end of the living room, two bold works of art—a Calder above the fireplace and a Miró on the side wall—add important elements of contrast while underscoring the use of geometry and form and incorporating the energizing accents of orange and cobalt blue at play throughout the house. While the upholstery is fairly neutral and muted, dashes of purple—the violet ikat on the Louis XVI–style chair, the lavender squares in the grid of the custom-colored rug, the amethyst footstools tucked beneath the console table, and the jolt of rich purple velvet on the tufted footstool by the fireplace—are woven into the room.

PREVIOUS PAGES: The center hall, with its dramatic fireplace, gives onto the living room, dining room, and staircase. The antique Swedish clock in the living room underlines the pale gray-blue and lavender Gustavian palette, which is sparked with unexpected touches of orange. OPPOSITE: The curlicues of the curtain fabric recall the loopy lines of the Frances Elkins chairs. ABOVE: Symmetry brings pleasing order to the living room, while the oval foot stool, curvaceous glass urns, and Calder painting balance the grid with circular forms.

Mixing geometrics may seem counterintuitive,
but establishing a cohesive rhythm of shapes
allows you the freedom to break out of the pattern.

In the dining room, graphic geometries abound: The lattice-like pattern of the flat-woven dhurrie rug is echoed in the mirrored trellis of the blue sideboard and the mirror above it, and in the carved X-backs of the dining chairs. Instead of crown molding, this room has lower, thinner picture molding, and we silver-leafed the ceiling and the walls above the picture rail, creating a shimmering, domelike effect. The reflective finish of the ceiling relates to the luminous yet textured Venetian plaster walls, just as the refined Swedish chairs and ornate crystal chandelier and sconces contrast dramatically with the rough-hewn pedestal table of reclaimed elm.

The brightest shades in our paint box come to the fore in the kitchen and adjacent family room. Although the kitchen is predominantly white, with an island of Absolute Black granite, the citrus-hued fabrics on the banquette, stools, and valance pop. The gridded concentric squares on the pillows and stool cushions are enlarged and emboldened on orange-and-white square bull's-eye pillows. The emphasis on geometry continues in the Chinese Chippendale chairbacks, the iron quatrefoils of the pendant lamps above the island, and even the subtle lines of the diamond tile backsplash. Thanks to judicious placement and variations in scale and hue, none of this shape-shifting is meant to hit you over the head; it just gives the scheme structure and resonance. If variety is the spice of life, it is especially important in a kitchen, where one is often faced with the relentless repetition of materials. (Think unmitigated stretches of cabinet fronts or a sea of subway tile.)

The blues become bolder in the family room, inspired by the Matisse-like cutout in the adjacent office. We covered the club chair and ottoman in a graphic pattern of hexagons, then revved up the saturation on a leather-topped ottoman with Yves Klein–blue fabric sides. We could get away with using such a strong color scheme on the upholstery because it is balanced by

PREVIOUS PAGES: Bold modern paintings by Calder and Miró are juxtaposed with antiques, a pale lavender-and-blue palette, and the tailored shapes of the living room furniture. OPPOSITE: The *X*'s of the Swedish chairbacks, the latticed mirrored doors of the sideboard, and the trellis of the dhurrie rug all play off one another.

The dining room is truly a study in contrasts, with the shimmer and sparkle of the silver-leaf ceiling, crystal chandelier, and sconces (family pieces) juxtaposed with textured Venetian plaster walls and the raw, rough-hewn wood table. The mirror and sideboard amplify the reflective quality of the crystal.

ROOMS WITH A VIEW

An enfilade is an architectural grace note, a classical arrangement whereby each room opens onto the next one through a series of doorways. The word *enfilade* comes from the French, meaning to string onto a thread—so the doorways are aligned like pearls on a necklace. Enfilades were a hallmark of many grand houses, and it is time their attributes were appreciated again.

- Doorways serve as frames for the composition of an enfilade, each one highlighting the view into the next room and building a sense of anticipation. Just as the right frame can elevate a work of art, so architectural casings can enhance and magnify a view. I think of an enfilade like a telescope: As you extend the scope, each section has its own distinct segment, but it also focuses and intensifies the end view as you look through it.

- If you are fortunate enough to have an enfilade of rooms, it is important to think about the view from one room to the next. You can shift gears in each space, creating a lively, staccato sense of contrast, or you can link them, for example, in a progression of color. In either case, the most important element

is the terminus, or focal point at the end. It's like the dot of an exclamation point. Here, the bold colors of the Calder painting above the fireplace neatly carry through the blues and oranges of the kitchen, while the dining room riffs on blues of a softer shade on the upholstery and rug.

- If you don't have an enfilade, it is worthwhile to create one where possible. Sometimes simply by moving doorways a foot or two, you can achieve this pleasing sense of order and symmetry, and greatly enhance your home's layout. If you are remodeling or building from scratch, an enfilade gives great spatial value. Instead of hallways, which are usually dead space anyway, rooms connected directly to one another provide a cozier feeling.

- Sometimes a window or doors to the outside are the terminus of an enfilade. This can be extremely appealing, as the eye is led through the house and out to a garden, a pool, or a leafy landscape.

- Windows along the sides of an enfilade introduce a play of light and shadow, highlighting elements within each room and adding a sense of expansiveness.

Adding layers of interest at different heights—from the chandeliers and their chains to the patterned valances, the pottery above the refrigerators, and bright cushions— helps break up the "sameness" of kitchen storage spaces.

Geometry adds texture to a mostly white kitchen. From the quatrefoil light fixtures over the island to the subtler patterns of the battens on the range hood and the diamond tiles on the backsplash, the details reflect the play of light and shadow. Splashes of orange appear on the barstool cushions, banquette pillows, valance trim, and even the cookware.

SOOTHING SWEDISH WITH BOLD PUNCTUATION

Gustavian blues, grays, and lavenders are enlivened with shots of bright orange and cobalt blue.
1. A beautiful painted linen on the curtains, "Volanges Métis Lin" from Manuel Canovas, echoes the leafy forms in the master bedroom. The taupe diamond piqué (left) from Rogers & Goffigon appears on the headboard and bedskirt; the pale blue textured linen from Pollack caps the long bolster pillow on the window seat. **2.** Vibrant cobalt blues saturate the family room, with Cowtan & Tout's textured chenille, "Sommières" (top right and bottom left), on the sofa and "Kyoto Shrine," a geometric embroidered linen (bottom right) on the armchair and ottoman. "Java Java" printed linen (top left), from Quadrille, and Zimmer & Rhodes's "Motiva" printed cotton (center) make graphic throw pillows. **3.** The elegant embroidered linen used for the screen in the dining room— "Honeysuckle" from Lee Jofa—sets the tone for that space. A pale blue textured linen from Hickory Chair upholsters the dining chairs. **4.** The concentric squares of "Ziggurat" printed linen from Quadrille juice up pillows and barstools in the kitchen. Claremont's whimsical "Butterfly" cotton marries blue and orange on the valance. **5.** The custom-colored needlepoint rug in the living room, "Mahoney" from Sacco Carpet, weaves together grays and lavenders in interlocking squares. Zimmer & Rhodes's "Heritage" paisley adds luscious detail on a pillow. **6.** A woven ikat from Lee Jofa, "Nirvana," updates a Louis XVI–style chair in the living room. "Scroll," a curlicued medallion embroidered on linen from Lee Jofa, feels young and fresh on curtains.

The blues go from
go-for-broke bold in the
family room to the palest
sky in the master bedroom
(FOLLOWING PAGES). The
bright Matisse cobalt
suits the energy of a family
space, while soft blues
create a feeling of serenity
in the bedroom. These
rooms capture the wide
range of moods this
versatile color can evoke.

the busy backdrop of the bookcases and lightened by the window-lined walls. Shimmering silver accents of the hammered lamp and garden stool also lend an important counterpoint.

This intensity gets dialed down to a whisper of blue in the serene master bedroom. Its architectural charms—the arched doorway, the snug built-in bookshelves and window seat, the quirky roofline, and the little window in the vestibule—are set off by the pale sky blue walls and quieter patterns. The room still has its shapely moments, however: the tall scalloped valance above the window; a wood-and-fabric trellis on the headboard (reiterated in the woven trellis of the throw); the dramatic, sculptural leaves of the bedside lamps; and the more delicate forest of leaves in the chandelier. The curtain fabric and scallop-embroidered bed linens pick up on those curvy, organic forms as well. Orange, blue's all-important companion in this house, makes an appearance even here, in the artwork, a bright spark in this soothing, tranquil haven.

Curves are subtly at play in the master bedroom, starting with the arched doorways and continuing onto the shaped valances and chairbacks, the leafy chandelier arms and curtain fabric, and the looped embroidery on the bed linens.

GEOMETRY LESSON

Details help carry through the message of geometric form and the distinctive color palette in this house.
1. We custom-colored the living room rug to create a grid of gray and lavender interlocking squares. Subtle square diamonds are woven into the tape trim finishing the hems of the armchairs, which have a hint of purple in their stripe. **2.** In the living room, a white outline emphasizes the wonderful silhouette of the painted console table's scalloped apron. Beneath it, a pair of shapely upholstered stools in violet leather echo the symmetry of the curvy gourd lamps. The brazen contrast of the modern painting keeps the color scheme from veering into the realm of the precious. **3.** A clear Lucite table doesn't compete with the mix of striped rug and geometric fabric in the family room. **4.** A wood headboard with wool insets in the master bedroom adds dimension. Leafy vines on the pillow shams almost seem to climb the lattice of the headboard. A sculptural lamp brings the leaves to three-dimensional life. **5.** Nailheads emphasize the soigné curves of this Louis XVI–style chair; the intricately carved frame contrasts with the more primitive ikat fabric. **6.** Even windows form a grid that inadvertently frames compositions. A simple French-pleat café curtain is all that's needed by the kitchen banquette.

2

3

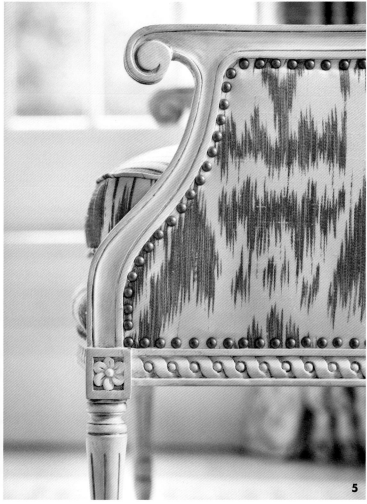

5

6

A WORLD IN BLUE
AND WHITE

Blue and white is a timeless, classic scheme; people have been falling in love with it for centuries. Before this project, I'd decorated blue-and-white rooms, but never an entire house. There are a wealth of fabrics and *objets* from which to choose in this iconic color combination, so the challenge of working with an extremely focused palette was a pleasurable one.

This plantation-style house with deep double verandas across the front is newly built in a beachfront community on the Gulf Coast of Florida. Sadly, the homeowners had lost their former country house in Pass Christian, Mississippi, to Hurricane Katrina.

Rebuilding after Hurricane Katrina in a new spot on the Gulf offered the wife an opportunity to explore her fantasy of a house decorated entirely in blue and white.

During that storm, they had to be airlifted out, and ended up coming to this Florida community to seek shelter. When everything had settled and they felt that it was time to rebuild, they decided to do so here. Luckily, they purchased this house early enough in the construction process that we were able to adjust some architectural elements to make it even more to their (and our) liking—closing off an open staircase, for example, and adding details such as pilasters, coffered ceilings, and built-in bookcases.

Blue and white is a natural choice for a house by the sea. In this case, the wife's love of decoration and design, combined with her cultivated eye, inspired us to take a more formal, elevated approach to our décor than the typical casual beach house might have required. This is a vacation home, true, but one appointed with lined curtains and valances, elegant canopy beds, fine porcelain, and mahogany furniture. Still, the toiles and ginger jars are relaxed by rustic apple, or Irish, matting and bleached sisal rugs on the floors, and by V-groove walls and ceilings in many of the rooms. The rugs are the perfect choice for a sandy beach house, and their rugged, natural texture is an essential counterpoint to the delicate florals of the fabrics.

The main rooms—living, dining, and kitchen—are actually on the second floor, placed there to take in the views. The living and dining room form one long rectangle, while the kitchen runs perpendicular to the dining room to create an L-shaped space overall. On the ground floor are the master bedroom, the library, and an enchanting bunk room for the grandchildren. On the third floor are two guest bedrooms and a TV/family room. A carriage house contains a small guest suite with a kitchenette.

PREVIOUS PAGES: The collection of blue-and-white porcelain in the foyer is a taste of the coming attractions. Different shades of blue—from the denim blue on the Klismos chair, to the gray-blue of the French mats on the engravings, to the midnight blue of the ottoman—all meld easily together. OPPOSITE: The deep two-story verandas on this plantation house, and other gracious architectural details, belie the home's new construction.

The entrance hall sets the stage for the house: A statuesque collection of blue-and-white porcelain sits atop an elaborately carved, white-painted William Kent table. The sisal rug and simpler Klismos-style chair, flirtatious French ottoman, and bold black-framed mirror hint at the juxtapositions that help contrast formality with beach-house ease.

In the living room, at least eight different fabrics are layered in a bower of blue and white. As the house was being built, and as we were developing our decorating scheme, we traveled to the site bearing suitcases filled with blue-and-white fabrics to audition in the space. It was essential to see them in situ, because different kinds of light can make some blues look greenish or gray, more harmonious or discordant.

The curtains unify the entire space with a beautifully drawn, detailed floral. Tall valances, trimmed with an elegant scalloped braid, graze the ceiling. The box-pleated valances emphasize the height of the room and, most important, conceal white woven matchstick blinds, which are crucial for modulating the glare in a climate where the sun is so intense. We even installed blinds outside, on the sides of the porch, to help temper the sun.

RIGHT: One of the ways I incorporate flat-screen TVs into room schemes is by treating them simply as a rectangle within a larger composition; here, flanked by Chinese ginger jars on pedestals and above vases on the mantel, the TV recedes.

FOLLOWING PAGES: We closed off what was planned as an open staircase to create a cozy seating area within the spacious living room. The scale of the Zuber wallpaper screen lends drama and adds complements of green.

BOTTICELLI
The Private World of Yves Saint Laurent & Pierre Bergé

Nearly every element is blue or white or both, but there are important points of relief in the dark wood side tables, and in the panel of antique Zuber hand-painted scenic wallpaper that the homeowners already owned and that we framed and hung above the sofa. The screen's dramatic scale, elegant gilded frame, and predominance of green provide a welcome complement. I also love the way the chunky linear braids of the rustic matting on the floors echo the V-grooves of the planked ceilings. Natural textures such as these help balance the refined fabrics and feminine patterns.

Behind the floral sofa, a tall painted and gilded console table helps create an informal demarcation between the living and dining areas. It can also be pressed into service during a dinner party as a buffet or sideboard. In the dining room, the chairs introduce two more patterns: the ticking stripe framed by the chair's inset back is a crisp counterpoint to the floral seats. The carved urn splats on the chairbacks suit both the fabric motifs and the magnificent Portuguese urn centerpiece on the table. When meals are not being served here, it's treated as a center table and stacked with books for more of a library-like feel.

The adjacent kitchen feels connected to the space as a whole, thanks to the white cabinets and the appliances camouflaged by cabinetry fronts. I generally like stainless steel, but in a house such as this one, where the kitchen is part of the living space, I prefer to minimize the workaday functions of the room. A spacious white-marble-topped island provides comfortable secondary seating, and beautiful antique Delft tiles—found on the Internet!—soften the expanse of wall above the range. As befitting a kitchen, the curtain fabric is continued on valances only, with white matchstick blinds and simple white café curtains below—my favorite approach to dressing kitchen windows. A pair of deep, cozy wing chairs (one antique and one carved to match); a painted chest that serves as a bar, with handsome oil paintings above it; table lamps in addition to pendants; and more apple matting on the floor make the room inviting and less kitchen-like—a place to sit down and relax.

The dining area is part of the great room, but it feels distinct thanks to the focal point of the giltwood gesso chandelier crowning a round pedestal table and chairs. The fabrics here are edited down to just two: a ticking stripe and a floral. A pair of dark wood pedestals with ferns add contrast, height, and a connection to the outdoors.

In an all-white kitchen, details become even more important: The trompe l'oeil painted ashlar blocks and scroll frieze on the curved range hood, the richly detailed tiles, and a row of glass-fronted transom cabinets showcasing blue-and-white porcelain all add warmth and personality to the space.

SETTING THE BAR

I pay particular attention to creating tablescapes on the flat surfaces of a room—whether on a mantel, coffee table, console table, or dresser. Setting up an informal bar on top of a table or cupboard, or on its own tray table or cart, is a gesture of welcome. The primary goal is not to create a shrine to alcohol—that's more for my own house—but to have the basics for drinks-making and entertaining at the ready while fashioning an attractive still life.

There's something sexy about a bar. For me, it evokes the black-and-white glamour of the old Hollywood movies I grew up watching, such as *The Thin Man,* or, more recently, *Mad Men* days of martinis and nightcaps.

Some general guidelines apply:

- Bottles of various spirits, often in an array of different shapes, sizes, and colors, create an interesting and varied skyline. Nowadays there are some particularly beautiful bottles designed for artisanal and small-batch liquors that are worth seeking out (provided you like their taste, of course). In a house as duotone as this one, such a still life gains even more punch (no pun intended) from the variety of technicolor mixers. They look best gathered on a generously sized tray, whether it is silver, lacquer, wicker, or some other material.

- The accoutrements of the bar also play an important role—horn or silver cups with bar spoons, stirrers, or toothpicks; a handsome bottle opener and corkscrew; linen or paper cocktail napkins; perhaps a crystal or silver ice bucket; or even a cocktail shaker and jigger. It used to be that one had a cup of cigarettes and a match striker; nowadays it's more likely to be small bowls of nuts or olives. I prefer a collection of varied pieces, perhaps antiques, rather than a bought and matched set, which doesn't look nearly as interesting.

- Make the bar tray part of a larger composition. Here, the pleasing symmetry of the urn lamps is echoed in the stone urns on pedestals behind them. Introducing lush colors into the blue-and-white scheme, the paintings are hung low, to help tighten the arrangement.

- I like using colored lampshades to add an extra layer of detail. We have an excellent lampshade maker who always insists on seeing the lamp base in person in order to determine the size, shape, and proportion of shade that will best suit the lamp. I never argue with her because this art is mysterious to me and many others, and I find it hard to get the right shade size without her guidance. It's also important to make sure the shade, not just the base, will fit comfortably on the table you've chosen.

ENDLESS VARIATIONS ON BLUE AND WHITE

In this house there are literally dozens of beautiful blue-and-white fabrics, and I don't think we even scratched the surface. Here, some up-close views of how we made them play nicely together: **1.** The flowering vines of "Nanou" chintz from Brunschwig & Fils climb the curtains and pillows in the upstairs TV/family room. The chairs are upholstered in the painterly strokes of "Plumettes" cotton (left), while the sofa is covered in "Bedford" textured chenille, both from Cowtan & Tout. **2.** "Bracieux Bleu Camïeux" from Pierre Frey (top left) is the enchanting toile used throughout the master bedroom. A bold linen ikat, "Delphos" from Cowtan & Tout, adds contrast on the bench. **3.** The finely drawn and very apt "Shell Toile" from Brunchswig & Fils (center) is worthy of its prominent place on the curtains in the living/dining room. One counterpoint is the "Felton" cotton ticking stripe from Cowtan & Tout. (left). The intricately layered loops from Samuel & Sons that trim the curtains are custom. **4.** A printed linen floral, "Arles," and a solid texture, "Montego," both by Cowtan & Tout, appear on benches in the entry foyer. The bold-striped outdoor fabric on the porch is "Commodore" from DeLany & Long. **5.** In the robin's-egg-blue guest bedroom, the canopy is a classic faded floral linen chintz, "New Chantilly" from Cowtan & Tout; it's lined in "Boxleaf" printed linen by Peter Fasano (center). **6.** The linen toile in the bunk room is "Rosedone Hall" from Hinson. The cobalt-blue-and-white textured cotton, "Colorado" from Pierre Frey, enlivens a slipper chair in the master bath.

new york state of mind
estado de ánimo de nueva york

sheer romance
romance puro

837

2

3

yarmouth blue

HC-150

buxton blue

HC-149

storm blue

5

6

The master bedroom is
pure romance, with
its intricate floral toile
lavished on curtains
topped by ruched valances,
on a regal coronet, and
on a tufted headboard.
The monogrammed
scalloped bed linens and
painted, tile-topped
tables infuse the space
with feminine grace notes.

With the public rooms concentrated on the second floor, the bedrooms on the first and third

floors can have more privacy. The bedrooms were truly a tour de force in the use of blue-and-white

fabrics: Each has its own shade of blue; its own style of upholstered headboard, half canopy, and

tiebacks; its own form of valance and curtains. For me, the master bedroom (prevous pages) is the

pièce de résistance, a reverie in blue and white with its intricately ruched valances and coronet,

gathered with tasseled cording. The more informal beadboard walls and sisal rug are an unexpected

but welcome foil to the elaborate bed hangings and curtains. Crisp white scalloped bed linens; the

bold, modern scale of the motif on the bench; and cobalt-blue tufted club chairs provide important

visual pauses. The formally framed Piranesis, with images of classical temples and the Pantheon,

helped us to keep the appearance of too much sweetness at bay.

The library, near the master bedroom on the first floor, takes a more tailored, masculine
approach to the blue-and-white scheme. The elegant sapphire-blue pattern on
the curtains suits the rich mahogany antiques in this room, while the solid upholstery,
sisal rug, and dark mats of the Audubon prints provide a quieter counterpoint.

A tale of two desks: Hers, tucked into a cubby off the kitchen (probably intended as a pantry) is white and cozy, topped by a charming fabric memory board tacked with favorite photos. His (opposite), in the library, is an antique drop-front secretary with a bouillotte lamp, obelisks, quill and horn accessories, and a leather chair.

The library is located adjacent to the master bedroom. Compared with the rest of the house, this interior is more formal, with darker woods; fine antique furnishings, such as a *secrétaire à abattant*; and handsome Audubon prints, which derive visual heft from dark taupe mats. This room's scheme is more sober, but it still has a gorgeous sapphire-and-white pattern on the curtains, soft shades of blue and beige on the upholstery, and a dressed-down sisal rug.

One of my favorite rooms in this house is the surprisingly sophisticated bunk room for the grandchildren. We created two-story bunks (four beds altogether) loosely modeled on the concept of Pullman railroad sleeping cars, except that these luxurious berths are fitted with twin mattresses; upholstered, inset, tufted headboards; and individually controlled sconce lighting. Each has its own TV built into the wall at the foot of the bed, with a box containing headphones

ABOVE: In the upstairs TV room (aka the kids' hangout), the curtains are motorized to close at the touch of a button for TV or movie viewing. Tufting helps break up the expanse of the sectional couch. OPPOSITE: On the second-floor porch, an outdoor sisal rug, rattan furniture, and a weathered wood table provide lots of texture, grounding the bold blue stripe on the upholstery.

and a remote control. We detailed the bunks with pilasters, grisaille-painted decorative borders, deep crown molding, curtains on delicate brass poles to provide darkness as well as privacy, and a small dust ruffle across the bottom. Despite the fact that this room is designed for children, the owner didn't leave anything out—it has the same beautiful window treatments, armchair, and serpentine-front chest that might appear in any other room in the house. *I'd* love to sleep here—imagine the fun the grandchildren must have bunking together!

For relaxing and lounging, there is a TV/family room near the guest bedrooms. I sometimes despair that TV rooms all seem the same, so I was pleased that here we agreed to arrange the walls like a gallery. We kept the cabinetry low, and surrounded the flat-screen TV with a series of paintings, treating the screen like just another rectangle in the composition of framed artwork, and thus diminishing its importance.

Outdoors, on the second-story porch, where everyone gathers to watch the sunset or catch the breeze, bold blue and white stripes offer a simpler coda to this color story. Rattan furniture, a teak table, and an outdoor sisal put the emphasis on natural textures, but intricately painted Portuguese planters and ceramics carry hints of the interior's play of pattern outside.

Ten-foot-high ceilings allowed us to create the polished version of a bunk room seen here. Inspired by Pullman sleeping cars, each bed has its own curtains that can be drawn for privacy, a reading lamp, and even a small TV fitted into the wall at the foot of the bed. The pilasters and painted frieze give the bunk beds a touch of architectural élan. The mahogany bowfront chest introduces an important note of contrast.

94

ABOVE: For a compact guest suite in the carriage house, an airy wrought-iron bedframe sans canopy introduces grandeur and structure without overcrowding. The painted ceramic medallion above the bed echoes the beautifully drawn chinoiserie toile on the tailored bedskirt and curtains. OPPOSITE: A carved plaster medallion of a different sort hangs in the master bath, above a shaped marble backsplash, elevating the view from the bedroom.

In a guest bedroom, an antique carved bed was extended to modern mattress proportions. The curtain valance is shaped in a gentle curve to let in more light and enhance interest across the wide expanse of windows; its curve is echoed in the canopy. The canopy fabric is the same as that of the bed, but pleated, it shows less of the white and more of the blue. Medallions covered in the same fabric serve as canopy holdbacks.

DETAILS IN BLUE
AND WHITE

Part of the fun of decorating this house was the wife's appreciation for each detail and her commitment to getting it right. **1.** These are not your typical bunk beds: Their frames are built to look like pilasters ending in plinth blocks, to break up the long expanses of wood, and the side panels are hand-painted with a grisaille border. Though we technically didn't need a dust ruffle (the beds are on wooden platforms, not box springs), the patterned one here (attached via the magic of Velcro) and the bed curtains in each compartment help soften the structure. **2.** An antique painted chest in the stair hall adds an unexpected touch of green. The large gilded mirror brings light into the hall and reflects the series of Piranesi prints lining the staircase. I designed the gold lamp base after a favorite form, the obelisk. **3.** Portuguese ceramic urns, used as planters on the porch, offset the bold stripes of the furniture cushions. **4.** In the powder room, we adapted a small antique chest found in New Orleans to serve as a vanity, adding a dark marble top and backsplash for contrast. We also raised the base to make it more comfortable to use as a sink. **5.** Dark wood pedestals in the corners of the dining room offer important contrast; for the same reason, we created the turned wooden votives on the table by milling and hollowing out large curtain finials. **6.** The range hood looks less monolithic with faux-painted ashlar blocks and an elegant scrolled grisaille frieze.

2

3

5

6

1

2

4

5

Intricately carved wooden frames, moldings called out in blue, and lush trims all complement the blue-and-white patterns elegantly.

1. The pattern on the dining chairs has a smaller, denser scale than the curtains, which suits the chair's size and helps the two patterns marry well together. **2.** Carved wooden brackets flanking the living room mantel hold Chinese ginger jars. Brackets seem to have fallen out of favor of late, but I still appreciate the way they add dimension to a display and serve as a kind of punctuation mark. **3.** We originally designed the living room curtains without a trim, but the finishing touch of this layered braid added an important element of texture and depth, which was especially helpful in breaking up the long run of curtains in the space. **4.** In the carriage house guest suite, a side chair is upholstered in the same toile de Jouy as the bed. The chair is new, but we had it custom-finished to enhance its character. **5.** Conversely, this dresser in the robin's-egg-blue guest room is an antique, but it was in such stylish disrepair that we had to touch up the detailing; we also marbleized the top in black paint, to create a stronger contrast. The key tassel echoes the wall color. **6.** No detail too small: The homeowner even managed to find blue-and-white umbrellas to place in the porcelain stand. Everything can be elevated with just a little thought, whether through coordinating monogrammed cocktail napkins or house stationery.

A MEDITATION IN GRAY

"Urban tranquillity" may sound like a contradiction in terms, but in this serene residence high above the Upper West Side of Manhattan, it is not. For the same couple's beach house in the Hamptons, we used lots of bright blues and coral reds, which suited the house's seaside environment, but here in the city, they wanted the space to feel sleek and modern. As smoky charcoal grays lighten into shades of oyster and pearl, the monochromatic palette creates a quiet, soothing environment, yet its layers of texture, pattern, and hue provide interest and important variation.

In the dramatic entrance hall, glossy slate-gray walls create a striking gallery-like backdrop for stark black-and-white paintings. Dark walls, especially in a small space without much natural light, create a jewel-box effect that showcases artwork and furnishings and heightens their impact. My father always believed that dark walls allow the corners of a room to disappear, making the space feel larger, and I agree. This apartment has perfect "level 5" paint finishes throughout (see page 165 to understand just how exacting, and expensive, this painting process is), and I don't think the husband has yet forgiven me. But I catch him staring at the walls, and I like to think he is secretly in awe of them.

This entrance hall leads in four directions—to the kitchen, dining room, living room, and bedroom hall. Originally closets lined its walls, which made it quite choppy. To streamline the space and clarify the traffic flow, we established a hierarchy of doorways: The closet doors became jib doors, which means they were painted to blend in with the walls, with no casings other than the continuation of baseboard along their bottom edge. The doorways that are passageways leading to rooms, on the other hand, we enlarged and called out in crisp white moldings. We darkened the red oak floors, and applied a vinegar treatment, twice, to remove the reddish tones.

PREVIOUS PAGES: A polished zebrawood console, a geometric mirror, translucent resin lamps, and glossy Benjamin Moore Satin Impervo–painted walls give the dark entrance hall a luminous finish. RIGHT: Doorways called out in crisp white trim help aid navigation; closet doors are fitted as jib doors to blend in with the walls. Slender benches upholstered in velvet add softness, as does the hand-tufted rug.

The living room is a long rectangle, almost a double cube, which is considered to be a pleasing proportion but is not necessarily easy to decorate. We arranged the furniture to make sense of the space, placing a pair of matching sofas back-to-back in the center to bisect the room. One faces toward a television area, and the other toward a conversation area. A console table sits between the two sofas, providing both a spot for a pair of sculptural wood lamps and a hard, luminous glass surface amid the sea of soft upholstery.

The walls shade into a paler gray here, melding into the wide expanse of sky on an overcast day. The trees of Central Park, seen through the west-facing windows and echoed by a tree in the corner, provide a leafy green counterpoint. The fabrics on the sofas and chairs evoke menswear suiting: wool windowpane checks and gray flannels. The play of geometry begun in the hall continues here with a Greek key motif on the rug and the diamond weave and tufting on the X-base bench.

In newer buildings such as this, ceilings are not dramatically high, so keeping furniture profiles low and sight lines open helps expand the sense of space. I also often raise doorway heights and hang curtains just below the crown molding to emphasize verticality. Plush fabrics such as velvet always make seating look inviting. Even the artwork suited our palette of grays.

Mixed metals—such as the brass-and-steel coffee table, and the lamp on the desk—disprove the imperative to use only one finish in a room. In this space, the cool grays might have seemed a natural fit for chrome, but in fact, brass curtain rods and picture lamps contribute warmth.

ABOVE: The flat-screen TV is framed by built-in bookshelves in the entertainment area of the living room. Flush-mounted doors sheathed in charcoal leather conceal electronics. OPPOSITE: In the entrance hall, chinoiserie-style jars are more unexpected and dramatic in black and white instead of the traditional blue.

What says drama in a dining room? Crossing over to the dark side adds oomph
and glamour, as seen in traditional wood dining chairs reinvented in glossy black,
a jet-black chandelier, charcoal sateen walls, and an ebony lacquer sideboard
with parchment-wrapped doors. A silver-leaf ceiling illuminates the inky palette.

While black and white might appear to be a limited palette, any old movie or photograph reveals that there are almost infinite shades of gray in between.

The wood tones of the furniture and floors introduce an essential element of warmth that keeps this composition in gray from feeling cold and clinical. While it might seem more natural to opt for nickel or chrome hardware and lighting with this scheme, we counterintuitively chose brass, for the same sense of warmth. The built-in cabinetry at the far end of the room gains interest from sleek leather-wrapped doors beneath the TV, which serve almost as a kind of wainscot.

The living room and dining room are connected by a large, open doorway, so we connected them decoratively as well. The same Greek key rug and gray linen curtains are used in both spaces, but the dining room walls are upholstered in charcoal gray wool sateen, and the furniture deepens into ebony and black lacquer. (Having had a black bedroom at age thirteen, I have an affinity for dark rooms such as these.) We took traditional wood dining chairs the homeowners already had and lacquered them black to match the square pedestal table, a welcome change from the standard rectangular or circular table. In black, the intricate fretwork of the chairbacks forms dramatic silhouettes, as does the black glass chandelier. Against all this darkness, the silver-leaf ceiling reflects and burnishes the light, an effect I find romantic and glamorous for dinner parties. You can go a little more over the top in a dining room, and perhaps should, since it's a room often in danger of being underused. Parchment-inset doors on the lacquer sideboard and the vertebrae of clear Lucite lamps lighten the tenebrous palette.

OPPOSITE: A play of trompe l'oeil geometry in the dining room: The graphic silhouette of the intricate carved chairback, emphasized in black lacquer, is layered over diamonds with three-dimensional realism in the painting behind it.

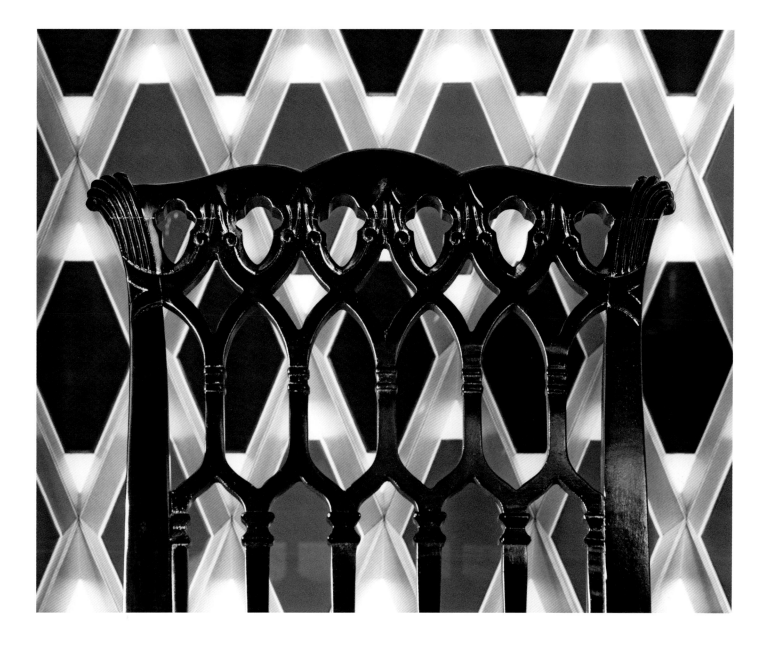

In the sitting room/office, the palette lightens and warms considerably, with shades of camel, taupe, and cream leavening the gray. The gray geometric squares of the carpet float on an ivory ground, and a taupe velvet sofa balances the black campaign desk and chair. Brass accents amplify that warmth, but it's the artwork that really makes this room: It's a saturated manifestation of the room's patterns and palette.

The grays become cloudlike in the master bedroom, creating an incredibly calming and serene space. Expansive views, paired with the quiet hues on walls, carpet, and bedding, dial down the clamor of the city to a hush. Intriguing pattern and texture emerge from the fabrics on the Roman shades, the chairs, and the pillows but are muted by the field of soft neutrals.

The harmonious palette that runs through this apartment not only is soothing, but also knits everything together in a cohesive whole.

GRAY MATTERS

A story told in black and white and gray, in all their many variations, draws warmth from camel, cream, and taupe in the bedrooms and baths. **1.** A faux bois wallpaper from Nobilis provides natural texture in the powder room. **2.** In the living room, starting from the center and working outward, are "Le Jardin," a woven tape trim from Samuel & Sons, used on the curtains; "Gainesborough" cotton velvet from Schumacher, on sofas; and a woven herringbone, "Melton" from Romo, and linen stripe, "Lateral" from Kravet, used on pillows.
3. This wonderful embroidered linen medallion pattern, "Mirador" by Cowtan & Tout, brings luxury to guest room pillows. **4.** Also in the living room, a distinctive geometric needlepoint, "Bohemian Rhapsody" from Schumacher, injects graphic pop on a tufted X-base bench, while echoing the rug in the entry hall. Ralph Lauren's classic wool suiting stripe "Regent Stripe" covers the sleek armchair near the television. **5.** We cut sections of Kravet's silk-and-linen embroidered "Chain Link" fabric (background) and applied them as a trim on the guest room's bedskirt. Like other rugs in the apartment, Stark's "Cyrus" is an interlocking geometric, here in shades of camel and brown.
6. From the top, Holland & Sherry's "Atacama" woven wool was used for the living room curtains; the firm's "Militaire" wool sateen covers the walls of the dining room; and Duralee's "Livingston" wool was used for throw pillows.

THE TEN COMMANDMENTS
OF KITCHEN DESIGN

1. It must look clean. This means using surfaces and materials that make it easy to spot dirt and are simple to maintain, such as light-colored counters (Calacatta marble) or uniform surfaces such as the Caesarstone we used here.

2. It must provide order for all the many things stored there. I find that a mix of solid doors and drawers (for foodstuffs, pots and pans, and other utilitarian elements) and glass-fronted cabinets (for plates, glassware, serving pieces, and other attractive items) works well in larger kitchens. In smaller, apartment kitchens, we often opt for all solid doors, for a sleeker look.

3. Storage space should not be defined too specifically. Your cabinetry and drawers need to be able to evolve and be adaptable to different uses. The exceptions are storage for pots and pans, and vertical slots for platters and trays.

4. If the kitchen serves as an eating space, or is part of a great room, it needs to feel welcoming, with comfortable chairs, or stools at an island. Banquettes and cushioned chairs add comfort.

5. The number of materials in a smaller kitchen should be limited, so it looks streamlined, not cluttered. In apartment kitchens, I tend to use the same material on countertops and backsplash. Slabs for the backsplash, such as the Caesarstone here, look sleekest.

6. If it's a large kitchen, a greater mix of materials should be used to help break up the expanse of cabinetry. In a sizable kitchen, I often prefer a tile backsplash. (Even if I use the same material, such as marble, on backsplash and counters, on the backsplash it will be in tile form, to provide more texture.)

7. It doesn't have to be white. White is light, clean, and airy, but it's also ubiquitous. Why not consider going richer and darker, as we did with the cerused-oak cabinets and cork floors in this kitchen? Strips of inset metal and sleek hardware add a bit of sparkle.

8. It should employ a variety of lighting sources: overhead, under-the-counter, pendants, strip lights. Kitchens are a place to have redundancy in lighting. Even here, overhead and pendant lighting should always be on dimmers.

9. It must have outlets galore. Some people like plug molds that are placed beneath the upper cabinets and have a long strip into which you can plug appliances anywhere; other people don't like seeing cords hanging down. Wherever you place them, err on the side of extra outlets.

10. Let the person who cooks have final say in the kitchen decisions. As my husband will be the first to tell you, I don't cook, so for me, these are all simply aesthetic issues. Real cooks may have different opinions.

LEFT: Geometric patterns—as subtle as the woven Roman shades or as pronounced as the rug and pillows—create a pleasing rhythm in the sitting room/office. ABOVE: Weathered faux bois wallpaper and a wonderful fish-scale mirror frame show that even the humblest powder room can be exalted by design.

Pale gray cocoons the master bedroom, with brushes of texture and pattern giving it depth. The bedside tables are vintage shagreen, while the embroidered waves of the Roman shades and the cut-velvet teardrops on the armchairs introduce organic forms. The box at the foot of the bed, designed to hold a flat-screen TV and mechanical lift, seems to be a necessary evil of modern living. We do our best to make it unobtrusive.

THE GEORGETOWN LADIES'
SOCIAL CLUB

C. DAVID
HEYMANN

Irwin Shaw

Ronald Searle

DETAILS FALL IN LINE

Whether fluid and scrolling or strict and rectilinear, geometric patterns play an important role in this design scheme. From classic, iconic forms (such as an interlocking Greek key and chain link), to more modern, amoeba-like swirls, to the subtle geometries of diamond quilting and tufted pleating, this apartment knows its lines.

1. Tightly spaced small nailheads accentuate the form of a tub chair in a guest bedroom. The coarse, rustic weave of the fabric contrasts with the polished wood and antiqued brass studs. **2.** The sinuous form of this armchair is echoed in the teardrop motif of the cut velvet fabric. Only the back is tufted, which I often prefer, so that dust doesn't catch in the seat cushion. **3.** The stepped steel stretchers on a pair of benches in the dining room instill a touch of sleek Deco shimmer. **4.** Deep button tufting on armchairs in the living room forms its own geometry. **5.** We added a couture level of detail to the tailored dust ruffle in the guest room by cutting a strip of chain-link embroidery from a separate fabric and applying it as a trim. **6.** A pinstripe bolster in taupe with corded piping and a button tuft brings a menswear touch to the guest room. Its regimented lines contrast with the more fanciful swirls of the embroidered pillows behind it.

2

3

5

6

1

2

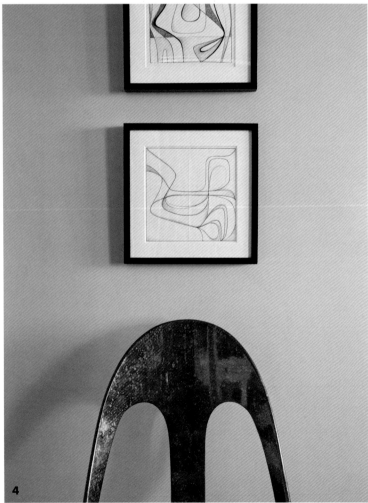

4

5

Form follows function—or does beautiful form enlighten function, making it more enticing? Details bestow another layer of elegance.

1. The hand-wrought brass hardware on this long Asian chest in the living room gives the piece a tactile element of artistry. **2.** An intriguing mix of materials and forms creates a distinctive silhouette for this lamp in the guest room. Bubbles of white resin are beaded with Lucite disks like a string of pearls. **3.** Design squared: A pair of brass cube cocktail tables in the study enlarges upon the square motif of the rug. The glass tops allow a layered view and keep the space feeling light and airy. **4.** Above the tall, swooping curve of a spoon-back chair in the living room, curvilinear sketches echo the chair's lines—and the room's black-and-white palette. **5.** A lattice of *X*'s called out in ivory makes a dramatic difference in this black frame chair in the wife's office.

6. A parchment and wood desk, also in her office, is topped with a modern yet whimsical lamp from Sandy Chapman: The glass cylinder can hold anything of one's choosing—the glass orbs we inserted look like elegant Ping-Pong balls.

GENERATIONS OF STYLE

I always find it fascinating to work with relatives. I've worked with sisters and good friends, but this is one of the few times I've worked with the children of clients. The blue-and-white beach house seen in the third chapter belongs to this homeowner's father and mother; the son resides in this turn-of-the-century house in New Orleans with his wife and young children. Invariably, the next generation tends to either mimic or rebel against their parents in a whole range of matters, not just decorating. Though this couple's tastes did not stray radically from that of the parents, their process was quite different. For first-time decorating clients, they were admirably decisive, and confident and adventurous enough design-wise to opt for sophisticated schemes such as the dark, tobacco-brown dining room.

PREVIOUS PAGE: The formal classicism of the entry hall is a perfect lead-in to the dining room. LEFT: The trim and tidy front of this early-1900s New Orleans house belies its spacious interior. OPPOSITE: The library is at the end of an enfilade connecting it to the living room and family room through large, gracious doorways.

The owners are enamored of warm, soft hues such as persimmon, rust, peach, and buttery yellows. These are colors that are not necessarily in fashion or "of the moment," but they are eternal and work beautifully here, and I give the couple credit for choosing a palette they genuinely love rather than being swayed by what's momentarily in vogue.

This is a charming house on a deep corner lot, and its modestly scaled front is deceiving: The building stretches back quite deeply to encompass a generous-size home with four bedrooms; a library, living room, and family room; and an attached guesthouse. When you walk inside, the eleven-foot-high ceilings announce that this is a house with a certain grandeur as much as it is a comfortable family home where the fabrics and palette were chosen to accommodate, if not camouflage, the fur of a blond Labrador retriever and the rough-and-tumble play of small children.

The architect, Michael Carbine, added many of his trademark flourishes, such as the raised-panel wainscoting and other elegant molding details. We sought to give this young family a clean palette and a streamlined backdrop for their life—a décor that had enough sophistication to suit them for decades to come while not aging them prematurely. We wanted the house to feel polished but not styled within an inch of its life. Everyone in my office envies this house—

it's the kind of inviting, cozy place that's nevertheless elegant and proper, a home where we young mothers could envision happily raising a family. It easily accommodates the pieces the couple already owned—such as the sofa, some of the tables, and the artwork—while embracing fine antiques and new furnishings.

The living room connects to the library and family room in a pleasing enfilade, with tall, gracious doorways that branch off to the dining room, kitchen, and foyer. We could have made each room a different color and called out the casings in sharply contrasting trim. Instead, we wanted to amplify the sense of space and continuity through color. The palette of russet, apricot, and taupe connects the span of three rooms, with different shades coming to the fore in each space. The most significant variation comes in the dining room, where dark lacquered walls create much more drama.

The foyer, like all good entrances, sets the stage for the house, though with a bit more rigor than the rooms beyond it. We chose a neoclassical console table (rather than one of the rococo antiques often associated with New Orleans) and placed a bull's-eye mirror on its lower shelf,

Textured and patterned fabrics, worn rather than polished woods, and sisal and multihued rugs make rooms more forgiving with young children.

in a sly evocation of a mirrored base. A pair of ornate urns, the large Egyptian print, and the gilded obelisk lamp underscore the classical allusions.

In the neighboring library, gorgeous embroidered curtains reach all the way to the ceiling, emphasizing its height and creating a lush backdrop for this simple, tailored room. I find that many young people are scared off by curtains, either worried that they will look too traditional or put off by the expense. Thankfully this couple was open to window treatments, which went a long way toward decorating each room.

The adjacent living room shares the same pale yellow walls as the library, but here the rust tones predominate. With large upholstered pieces that are all fairly neutral, it's the pillows, throws, and smaller accents—such as the ikat-covered ottoman and the pleated card-table chair covers—that introduce notes of color. The room strikes a nice balance between formality and informality. At one end, a pair of antique cabinets and mirrors anchors the room with traditional symmetry. Elsewhere, plump, comfortable upholstery; a dressed-down sisal rug; and artwork propped up on the mantel give more relaxed cues. The seating is organized around the fireplace, with its original mantel and Saint Laurent marble surround, but the long proportions of the room also allowed space for a card table at one end and a console and chairs at the other. Two of the couple's favorite artists are well represented in this room, with paintings both framed and unframed propped up against furniture as well as hung.

PREVIOUS PAGES: The same color scheme is carried through to the living room, but with taupe curtains and upholstery and persimmon accents. OPPOSITE: Intricately embroidered curtains with an almost New Orleanian fleur-de-lys pattern in the library create an elegant backdrop for simple antiques the couple already owned. Items such as the gun case on the bench and family photos give the room personal resonance.

When designing with young children and a large dog in mind, you don't want to forgo personality or practicality, and these homeowners never did. There's enough punch to make this room personal, with graphic pillows on the sofas, leopard-print-stripe chairs, and saucy pleated chair skirts, but it's measured, so that it doesn't overwhelm the artwork or the overall scheme. The curtains are a solid neutral with a terra-cotta fringe—the same colors that appear on the library curtains, but with the polish of box-pleated valances rather than rustic bamboo shades.

An eclectic little powder room tucked beneath the stairs and the chic espresso-hued dining room demonstrate the power of a dark palette. Both daringly contrast with the adjacent rooms on the first floor. With its glossy claret walls and unexpected black vanity, the tiny jewel box of a loo

OPPOSITE: The main seating group in the living room is arranged around the central fireplace, which allowed us space for a small game table area off to one side. Fun fern-frond pillows in lavender and orange add zip to the leopard-stripe side chairs.
ABOVE: The plaid loveseat on the other side of the living room is punched up with graphic scrollwork pillows. The library can be seen through the doorway.

THE JEWEL BOX

The concept of turning a small, dark, awkward space into a jewel box is decorating alchemy at its best. Often these grandeur-challenged spaces, to put it nicely, are powder rooms or older baths, but they can also be cramped, dim dens; former maid's rooms; or musty attics. Fortunately, with a little help, it's possible for them to be transformed, phoenix-like, into stunning libraries, charming guest rooms, and cozy home offices. Even closets, pantries, and cloakrooms can rise well above their station when treated with a little TLC. (See the pantry turned home office on page 90.)

The fun of these spaces, with their quirky eaves, antiquated fixtures, or diminutive scale, is that, ironically, with so many constraints to contend with, you are liberated to take a no-holds-barred, more whimsical approach to decorating. It's possible to splurge on luxurious materials because you're using such a small quantity of them. The deep color, wild wallpaper, or ornate tile you couldn't bear in a large room becomes a delightful flight of fancy in a powder room in which you spend only short amounts of time. You might mirror the whole space, or wallpaper the ceiling, or have a mural painted on the walls. Seek out ornate fixtures, or a couple of yards of fantastic fabric, or vintage crystal knobs. This is a place where you can afford to go for broke—or baroque.

You can cover every surface of an attic room in an intricate toile and you won't notice all the odd angles in the roofline. You can choose one overscaled piece of furniture or a dramatic light fixture to make a statement. You can collage old photos or maps from floor to ceiling.

I've mentioned before that, contrary to expectation, dark colors can make small rooms look bigger. The darker hue helps the corners of the room or an irregular roofline disappear, so the impression is simply one of color. If you lacquer the walls or use a glossy paint, as we did in this claret-colored powder room tucked beneath a staircase, the luminous reflections add richness.

Indulge in a variety of materials: Here we made an undistinguished, abbreviated vanity look special with high-gloss black paint and a Saint Laurent marble top that echoes the living room fireplace. The ornate brass faucet and taps, wall-mounted to save space, stand out against the black marble, and the single, swagged curtain pulled to one side is luxuriously fringed. (One swag is all there was room for, but it also looks far more dramatic than a pair of café curtains.) Instead of settling for compact generic light fixtures, we found smaller-scale library sconces with detailed brass back plates and capped them with Venetian half shades. In a large room, you sometimes can't manage to dot every *i*, but in a small space, you can attend to every detail.

Treat a neglected stepchild with princely riches (at least as far as attention goes) and you will be rewarded with a royal space that might end up being one of your favorite places in the house.

ABOVE: Unexpected touches of red, from the lamps to the picture mats, illuminate the deep cocoa walls of the dining room. Glossy lacquered walls and dramatic window treatments make the room feel finished even as the homeowners build their collection of art. OPPOSITE: A grid of gilded frames and red mats elevates a series of architectural prints, and connects to the red outlines in the rug and the paneling of the wainscoting.

The butterscotch-and-apricot palette that unites much of the first floor is warm, sunny, and welcoming—and blends well with the family's blond Labrador retriever.

feels both larger and richer than it would if it were simply white. Accents of gold in the compact library sconces, ornate brass faucet, gilded mirror, and curtain fringe emphasize an opulence that belies the room's diminutive square footage.

The dining room is the most formal, carefully composed space. It's all about graphic shapes, from the fantastic dhurrie rug that weaves together the brown-and-red scheme, to the curvy tentacle-like arms of the giltwood chandelier, to the bold ikat pattern on the curtains, to the spiraled lamps on the buffet. The curvaceous dining chairs are upholstered in dark brown leather, with the surprise of textured red velvet on the backs, which helps prevent them from disappearing visually into the brown of the table and walls. With the plush velvet, glossy walls, and the mystery and intimacy conjured by dark spaces, this is a very sexy room.

To walk into the family room is to come back into the light. This room is lined with windows that bathe its buttery walls in sunshine. An intriguing Indian paisley printed linen in shades of tangerine and light mustard gives this pale, sorbet-hued room a wonderful sense of character. Even though this is where the TV resides, the room feels calm and collected. A broad range of styles are encompassed here, from the New Orleans Louis XV carved commode beneath the TV and a tailored Louis-Philippe dresser, to the white Gothic side table, bamboo side table, and chinoiserie mirror. Amazingly, the couple already owned this Oushak rug, which works perfectly in this room. Its washed palette ties together the apricot velvet sofa, textured club chairs, pink Fortuny bergère, and paisley curtains. Sultanabads and Oushaks are often my first port of call when I am looking for a rug, so I was thrilled that we had such a beautiful one to employ here.

OPPOSITE: Curtains reach to the eleven-foot-high crown molding, emphasizing the height of the rooms. We layered in bamboo blinds in the family room and library, contrasted with more formal valances in the living room. FOLLOWING PAGES: The family room, with its soft velvet sofa, chenille club chairs, fireplace, and TV, is definitely the place to cozy up and relax, yet it also maintains an air of elegance through the mix of fine textiles such as the rose Fortuny fabric on the bergère, the large-scale paisley linen curtains, and the Oushak rug.

A COMPLEMENTARY PALETTE

The rusts, golds, and orange-y reds of the first floor are complemented by fresh greens in the kitchen, playroom, and upstairs bedrooms.

1. Subtle touches of the animal kingdom animate the living room, with a floral-and-bird printed cotton (center) from Schumacher; the mini leopard-print chenille is from Cowtan & Tout. **2.** Though softly colored, the Moroccan printed paisley linen from Quadrille is large enough in scale to make a strong impact on the eleven-foot-long curtains in the family room. **3.** In the living room, a neutral geometric pattern from Cowtan & Tout woven on the sofa (top) is sparked with a bold woven ikat from Brunschwig & Fils on the ottoman and silk stripe pillows from Claremont. The luxurious tasseled fringe from Samuel & Sons elevates the taupe curtains and box-pleated valance. **4.** Bright shades of chartreuse and lime in the master bedroom are quieted with gray and taupe textiles. A printed linen floral from John Rosselli on the curtains ties the scheme together. The linen ikat (bottom right) from Schumacher on the dust ruffle and European square pillows brings modern freshness to the room. The graphic woven pattern (bottom left) on the tufted bench and the geometric woven fabric on chair pillows (center) are both from Schumacher. **5.** The distinctive cartouche pattern of the dining room's wool dhurrie rug, "Alhambra" by Todd Alexander Romano, echoes the sculptural shape of the chandelier and was custom-colored to echo the room's scheme of brown with touches of red. **6.** The statement-making (and room-making) fabric in the library is Cowtan & Tout's embroidered linen medallion, which beautifully weaves together shades of red and orange. A detailed woven linen from Schumacher (bottom left) and silk stripe from Coraggio Textiles form more linear patterns on pillows.

2

3

grant beige

bennington gr

manchester ta

bleeker beige

greenbrier be

5

6

Upstairs in the master bedroom there is a shift in palette, to a refreshing light apple green, which complements the warmer shades in the downstairs rooms. I did a show house in 2007 in which we used a pale lime scheme for a bedroom. The walls were so horribly bright that we had to cut the paint with white and redo it, and then we ended up with a beautiful room. This time around, I was happy that I already knew this would make an ideal color for a bedroom, both soothing and piquant. The curtains and shaped valances are done in a green floral on a gray ground, which gives them a more timeless quality compared to the kicky acid green throw and vibrant ikat chevron euro squares and dust ruffle. The Swedish painted dresser, the carpet, and the marble lamps pick up the taupey gray. This is an asymmetrical, angled room, so the green-on-green furnishings and walls help draw attention away from its slightly quirky shape, and the largely monochromatic scheme makes the space feel restful.

In the end, what we all love about this house is exactly this balance—between timeless and youthful, classic yet fresh, grown-up but still growing.

ABOVE: Zesty chartreuse and lime in the bedroom are tempered by accents of gray in the curtain fabric, carpet, and painted dresser. OPPOSITE: For those with a sense of humor, the watercolors depicting New Orleans cemeteries could be construed to mean "Rest in Peace"—preferably not the eternal kind.

A SHARED PALETTE, DISTINCT DETAILS

With a singular color scheme spread across three rooms, the dressmaker details on pillows, curtains, and chairs help differentiate the personality of each room. **1.** At first we chose a darker gimp trim for the dining room chairs, but we realized that lightening up the braid would show off the chairs' curvy lines. **2.** The distinctive silhouette of this lamp is emphasized by its Greek key detailing in gold. A cut-velvet Holland & Sherry fabric on pillows layers in another geometric pattern. **3.** Flirty box-pleated, short-skirted slipcovers on the cane-back card table chairs relieved a sea of brown at one end of the living room. A back pleat makes them easy to slip on and off. **4.** We covered frame chairs belonging to the homeowners in a sprightly golden diamond lattice fabric. The curved bowl on the table is actually a cheese grater, also trimmed in a Greek key pattern. **5.** Appliquéd scroll-work pillows and an ikat-covered ottoman, both in rust, aren't jarring because their coloring and scale relate, yet they're different enough from the airier plaid of the loveseat for all to work together.

6. The painting over the living room chest, done by one of the couple's favorite artists, is a portrait of their house. The blues and greens of much of the artwork complement the yellow and red tones of the fabrics.

2

3

5

6

3

6

Each humble seam offers an occasion to add a special finishing touch, whether nailheads, tape trim, piping, or fringe.

1. The form of the wrought-iron lamp subtly echoes the paisley medallion on the family room curtains and the embroidered curtains in the library across the way. **2.** A lattice-textured fabric was made into cushions and arm covers that follow the curves of a caned chair. **3.** Marble column lamps pick up on the grays of the Swedish dresser and the curtain fabric in the master bedroom. **4.** The luminous colors of Fortuny fabrics make them a worthy indulgence when the budget allows. Here, closely spaced antiqued nailheads pick up on the silvery tones of the fabric on this carved French bergère. **5.** Bamboo shades have a wide range of tones, from greens to reds to browns, that isn't entirely predictable, but I like them in all their variations. They work as well with the gray-and-green floral curtains in the bedroom as they do with the brick reds and soft oranges downstairs. **6.** Most of the "solid" fabrics we select are enriched with a texture. The diamond-weave textile on the chairs in the master bedroom is edged in a darker twill tape. Both chairs and ottoman have waterfall skirts, which means there is no piping or seam below the cushion; the skirts fall straight to the floor, giving the pieces a more modern, streamlined look.

SEASIDE STYLE

The couple who lives here had been looking for a house in the Hamptons for quite a while when they found this one in a good location. Some of its details seemed like shortcomings, but as design aficionados, they were up to the challenge of fixing them. Though it is a relatively new house, they put their own stamp on nearly every room, changing all for the better.

The exterior needed a clearer sense of entry and stronger architecture. The single front door got lost in the expanse of clapboard siding, so the new owners added a window-lined vestibule with built-in benches. This not only serves as a prettier version of a mudroom, but

also greatly enhances the façade, making the entry more prominent and better balanced between the window bays. This anteroom is the prologue to the decorative narrative that follows, with its blue-and-white striped and patterned pillows, white beadboard window seats, bamboo blinds, and blue-and-white Chinese porcelains.

The two-story entrance hall was completely open to the upstairs, which can create noise as well as privacy issues. Just as good fences make good neighbors, sometimes a few walls make for family harmony. Adding a wall behind the stairs at the wife's inspired suggestion sequestered the bedrooms from the foyer and gave the entry some much-needed character and definition.

The lack of walls was also an issue with the open great room and kitchen, with no separate living room (one of my personal pet peeves). For anyone who hopes to entertain, or who values a

ABOVE AND OPPOSITE: The addition of a window-lined vestibule created a more architecturally distinctive and balanced façade. Welcoming cushioned beadboard benches with plush pillows, a rugged slate floor, and beautiful porcelain planters and urns provide a sophisticated take on a mudroom/entry.

place for quiet conversation and classic design, I find a separate, walled living area essential. We inserted a wall between the kitchen and what is now the living room, which also gave us the opportunity to line the room in bookshelves. Even in the age of iPads and Kindles (and I use both), I don't consider a house to be a home without books.

The living room became a more intimate, cozy space with its millwork, coffered beadboard ceiling, and soft, inviting upholstery. There are at least nine different fabrics in this room, but it doesn't feel too busy because many are solids, simple stripes, windowpane plaids, or classic checks. We used a more detailed floral cartouche on the bergère, which befits its unique silhouette, and on throw pillows.

There is a lively mix of finishes in this room—from the mahogany campaign table, to an ebonized bobbin table, to a sculptural painted pedestal table in the corner, to a Chinese table beside the large checked armchair. The bamboo blinds add texture and pick up on the wood tones in the room.

If the living room has a somewhat relaxed, casually elegant feel, the dining room is our tour de force. The midnight blue ground of the Gracie hand-painted wallpaper, with its landscape of silvery white flowering trees, creates a very dramatic backdrop. Its deep tones are echoed in the navy leather chairs and espresso wool sateen curtains, while the brown-and-white checked fabric on the chairbacks

The living space was originally completely open to the kitchen. We closed it off and wrapped the room in bookshelves for a more intimate feel. The wide brass picture lamps atop each shelf, combined with the palette of blues, give the room a slightly nautical air. FOLLOWING PAGES: The dining room wallpaper inverts the traditional palette of blue on white, seen on the Chinese porcelains, to dramatic effect.

WALL TO WALL

As the largest surface in any room, walls are its foundation. How they are treated and what we can do to make them special are important considerations in any project.

My favorite wall treatment is probably a "level 5" paint finish. This means the walls are skim-coated with plaster, sanded very smooth, and then painted in several coats, with sanding between each coat. The paint is rolled on, then brushed out with a fine brush, so that each coat is perfectly smooth, with no orange-peel texture. We generally use an eggshell finish or Benjamin Moore Satin Impervo paint for this, or we can add a decorative finish if desired. If I do a glaze, it has a tight, uniform texture that doesn't call attention to itself. Clients are sometimes taken aback by the time and expense of doing level 5 walls, but once they see the difference, they have no regrets.

Lacquered walls require even more preparation and layers of paint, but the final effect is stunning. In dark spaces or in dining rooms, lacquering beautifully amplifies the light. If you spray it on, as some painters do, the paint can sometimes sag or droop, and I've seen it take as many as fourteen coats to get the finish right. People once used car paint to achieve a lacquered effect. It dries quickly, but is no longer used because it is terribly unhealthy for the painters. The best paints for lacquering come from Fine Paints of Europe. If the walls need a little more gloss, I will often do a final clear coat.

I also love to use wallpaper or to upholster walls with fabric to make them more special. Upholstery is perfectly suited to private spaces such as bedrooms, where it helps insulate them from noise. I tend not to use wallpaper in larger spaces such as living rooms, where I feel it can distract from the artwork, but I do sometimes upholster living room walls in a subtle fabric such as a silk damask. My preferred method is the way J. Edlin Interiors does it: by creating a stretcher frame around each wall, so the fabric is stretched into place, with bunting beneath it. Gluing fabric onto walls can discolor the material, or the glue can dry out and peel off over time, and it's hard to get clean edges. Fabric can also be paper-backed and applied like wallpaper. That is the only way I would recommend using fabric in a bathroom, because it's sturdier, longer-lasting, and less germ-y.

I'm more likely to use wallpaper in secondary spaces, such as bathrooms, stairways, and halls, where it adds interest to an overlooked space and isn't as big a production to change if desired. One notable exception is dining rooms. There, Gracie hand-painted wallpapers are often my ideal (as in the dining room opposite). Not only are they exquisitely detailed, but you can alter the coloration and various elements, adding more birds, butterflies, and so forth. I also work with an artist, Franklin Tartaglione, who does hand-painted murals. When the murals are painted on canvas, the homeowners have the option of framing them or taking the murals with them if they move.

In the family room, the play of geometry is subtle but striking, with windowpane plaid walls, a striped rug, and tongue-and-groove ceilings. Even the cushions of the sectional sofa and the channel-stitched ottoman underscore the grid.

seems unexpectedly simple yet chic. We had the Bakshaish rug, a classic Persian pattern that is typically camel-colored, woven in a darker, richer shade of tobacco. Having touches of brown added to the branches in the wallpaper tied the navy and brown scheme together more tightly. To elevate the architecture, we introduced a paneled wainscot and a deeper crown molding, and removed a window seat in the bay, where a marble-topped mahogany cabinet now stands. A pair of demilune tables flanking the back window add shimmer painted in silver and navy and topped with blue marble we found.

In the family room, the blues get paler and frostier, but camel and ivory warm them up. A windowpane lambswool fabric on the walls (the wife jokes that she has never met a wall she wouldn't like to upholster) creates a cozy, inviting feel, and its grid offers a neatly graphic backdrop for large-scale paintings of farms that echo the fields outside. The striped rug parallels the direction and feel of the beadboard ceiling and, like the throw pillows, weaves in shades of dusty blue and taupe.

The family room's doors originally led outside; then the owners added the expansive sunroom, which has quickly become one of their favorite places to hang out. The family room has more of a cozy "indoor" feel for fall and winter, but it bathes in the glow from the summery sunroom. Both spaces have a fireplace so they can be enjoyed year-round.

In a sunroom lined with windows like this one, with beautiful, verdant views, the instinct is not to curtain them. But a room this large and this white would have felt too bare and cold with undressed windows. Simple but full chambray-blue curtains and warm bamboo blinds provide an important anchor. The husband loves hardware, and he chose the distinctive cremone bolts (the vertical locking bolts) on the casement windows. There is a great deal of blue in this room, but it feels serene because it is solid, without much pattern, taking its soft hue from the deeper periwinkle painting on the wall (see page 2). The walls, ceiling, and floor are all white beadboard and planks, so we tinted the walls a pale greige. Organic textures in the chunky braided sisal rug, the bamboo blinds, and the raw driftwood-like coffee table ground the room. Contrasting darker wood pieces, such as the barrel-back chairs and trestle table, and the deeper indigo blues of the ginger jar lamps

OPPOSITE: The pocket doors once led outside; the family added an expansive sunroom that creates the feeling of indoor-outdoor flow. FOLLOWING PAGES: The sunroom is washed in monochromatic blues contrasted with the rugged textures of the braided sisal rug and bamboo blinds. The woods, ranging from bleached and weathered to polished and dark, and the greens of the foliage, are an essential counterpoint.

OUT OF THE BLUE, A FLOWERING PALETTE

You don't have to have a house near the sea to love blue—shown here in a wide range of patterns, hues, and textures. **1.** Schumacher's "Katsugi" floral-printed linen (bottom), on an arched-frame chair and pillows, stands out among the subtler solids and geometrics in the living room. Pierre Frey's "Hossegor" woven fabric (center) is used on throw pillows with a white brush fringe. "Tulip," a hand-blocked wallpaper (top) from Galbraith & Paul for Holland & Sherry, elevates a butler's pantry.
2. This custom, hand-painted wallpaper from Gracie uses silver leaf for a showstopping backdrop in the dining room. **3.** Ralph Lauren's "Tabley House Floral" is the pretty wallpaper in the master bathroom. "Dear Lily" (center) is embroidered on a linen ground from Scalamandré, and used on sofa pillows and a lampshade in the master bedroom.
4. A geometric handwoven rug, "Dantsu" from Beauvais, defines the seating area in the master bedroom. The Fortuny hand-block print "Cimarosa" appears on the chaise and pillows in the sunporch off the bedroom. **5.** An elegant damask pattern is printed on grass cloth on the Stroheim wallpaper in the large guest room. **6.** From top, a custom handwoven wool carpet from Elizabeth Eakins, "Flame Stitch," is the stair runner and rug in the entry foyer. "Ionian Sea Linen" grass cloth wallpaper from Ralph Lauren tops the wainscot on the second-floor landing and hall. Clarence House "Delft," a bold linen floral, forms the curtains in the entrance hall. Carleton V "Strié Damask" cotton velvet appears on the window seat cushions in the vestibule.

2

3

5

6

A mix of beadboard, flat- and glass-front doors; latches and cup pulls; blue and white cabinets; and marble and stainless-steel counters gives a large kitchen visual variety.

and the saturated cerulean painting energize the floating sky blues and beiges in this airy space. The blue of the curtains and upholstery is also the perfect foil for all the green outside the windows. Is it any wonder that this is the room to which everyone gravitates?

When they're not gravitating to the kitchen, that is. The room the couple started with was, quite frankly, a disappointment—it was trying too hard to be "hip" and not hard enough to be functional and inviting. Now crisp white cabinets—with a pleasing variety of beadboard- and glass-fronted cabinet doors and flat and paneled drawers—look clean and orderly but not antiseptic. In a kitchen of this size, it's important to vary the door fronts, hardware, and finishes to keep things interesting. The vast island is a pretty periwinkle blue topped with statuary marble, while heavy-gauge stainless-steel counters flank the range. A custom-made steel shelf deep enough to hold plates sits beneath warming lamps installed in the vent hood, a clever idea of the wife's; a pot-filler faucet tucks in there as well.

The cabinetry reaches up to the ceiling, with a rolling library ladder making it easy to access the uppermost cabinets. The wife is a plate-aholic, so the wall of full-depth storage serves as a home for her wonderful collection of serving- and tableware. It also frames the TV with enough colorful elements that the screen almost fades from view. In the window-lined breakfast area, a generous round table features a carved apron that coordinates with the comfortable yet elegant barstools. So often barstools are hard perches that don't invite lingering; upholstered backs and seats make all the difference.

Upstairs, the story in blue and white continues. Blue has long been considered the most soothing color for bedrooms because it evokes water and sky. Here, as in the sunroom and kitchen, it tends toward the periwinkle side of the spectrum. Originally, we found the L-shaped master

OPPOSITE: Touches of fabric—ruffled pendant shades, print valances, breezy café curtains, and awning-stripe cotton rugs—add a welcome dose of softness to the hard finishes in a kitchen. FOLLOWING PAGES: A generous-size island in blue provides a central anchor for the large space.

bedroom with its quirky peaked ceiling to be a somewhat challenging space, but we helped make sense of it by adding a strong crown molding to replace a featureless picture molding, and by building in low cabinetry to line the alcove on one side, with recessed bookshelves opposite. The cabinets were made to the wife's specifications for storing her linens.

The homeowners enclosed what had been a small porch to create a window-lined sitting area, and we hung wide curtains flanking the doors to the porch so that the light could be blocked when needed for sleeping. A beautiful geometric area rug from Beauvais helps anchor a cozy seating area within the main room and relieves the large expanse of wall-to-wall carpeting. The bedroom furnishings range from sweetly traditional (such as the painted French bergère upholstered in a delicate floral lattice) to clean-lined modern (the goatskin parchment coffee table). A gorgeously detailed Fortuny fabric covers the headboard and bedskirt, balanced by a simple tailored ivory canopy outlined in a crisp tape trim border. As in all the blue-and-white rooms, the mahogany desk, chair, and bedside tables help ground the paler hues.

In the master and guest baths, wallpaper and fabric wrap the walls with dense overall patterns that read almost as textures. Pristine white Thassos marble was selected for slab counters and

backsplashes, tiled shower and tub enclosures, and two-inch-wide herringbone floors. The elegant Lefroy Brooks fittings include, in the master shower alone, an overhead shower, a hand shower, and a rain dome, for luxurious soaking.

While continuing the color scheme, each guest bedroom has its own distinct personality. The largest is papered in a sophisticated damask-printed grass cloth, with two double beds nestled beneath a soaring beadboard ceiling. This room also has a ladder up to a loft hideaway, where the owners hope their future grandchildren will one day sneak away to play games and read. The room had its quirks, however, with an uneven roofline and a window abutting a corner. Treating the three windows as one—with simple curtains featuring a geometric trim on the leading edge, and a single bamboo shade—drew attention away from their asymmetrical placement.

OPPOSITE: A porch off the master bedroom was enclosed to create a sitting room, Like the sunroom downstairs, it is lined with windows for panoramic views.
ABOVE: Low cabinets were designed to precise dimensions for storing the family's linens; their generous depth provides a display space for art and *objets*.

Serene periwinkle blues envelop the master bedroom, where a bit more pattern is welcome. Floral pillows and chairs, a deeper tone-on-tone Fortuny fabric on the bed, the geometric rug, and porcelain lamps layer patterns of varying scale and density to beautiful effect. Even the books are in keeping with the palette: The wife says, "I have so many books that it was easy to edit the focus to just blue ones in here."

RIGHT: In all the guest bathrooms, bathers can luxuriate in a rain dome, a regular shower, and a hand shower. OPPOSITE: A guest room in the carriage house has the snug, cozy feel of a woodland bower. The intricate toile, with its deep brown ground, also helps camouflage the many intersecting planes of the roofline and eaves.

Nailheads became a subtle motif in this room, both in the old-fashioned leather-trimmed steamer trunks placed at the foot of each bed and outlining the custom-made upholstered headboard frames. We even studded the orblike chandelier. The artwork introduced touches of green into the room, which we carried onto the European shams and a bright grass-green velvet throw pillow. The Elizabeth Eakins rug helps weave in the colors of the room.

Above the pool house is a true hideaway, a wonderful little bower covered in a luscious blue and brown toile de Jouy. Its deep color and enveloping pattern create the feeling of a refuge, wrapping all the angles and eaves of this attic-like aerie. The built-in window seat offers an inviting nook for curling up with a book. No detail has been overlooked: The design on the fabric Roman shade on the small window matches up perfectly with the wall upholstery above it—the genius of our curtain workroom, Anthony Lawrence Belfair, and wall upholsterer, J. Edlin, working together. The plaid chair and pillows outlined in corded trim and brushed fringe; the tufted window seat; the charming bolster pillows; the gooseneck sconces—all add flourishes that contribute to the sense of delight, to the feeling that even in the smallest of spaces everything is done just right.

A lush, large-scale damask, screened onto textured grass cloth wallpaper, helps bring the cathedral-ceilinged guest room down to size. Touches of grass green punctuate the icy blues in this room.

A TIMELESS DUO: BLUE AND WHITE

The solid blue and patterned blue-and-white fabrics in this house range from elegant velvets and Fortuny damasks to casual paisleys and workhorse plaids. As these images show, there's no need to worry about blues matching exactly—it's the mix of tones and textures that makes it interesting.

1. In the front entrance hall, we had this bench custom-built and the bolster sewn into place, so it won't roll off and can serve as an arm. The gorgeous Fortuny fabric on the pillow was the homeowner's.
2. The couple collected blue-and-white porcelains, and we expanded upon their collection in the dining room. Details on the demilune tables are called out in silver paint. **3.** The entry hall was originally large, spare, and a bit cold; we added curtains in a vivacious pattern to soften and warm it up. **4.** On the barrel-back chairs in the sunroom, carved and polished mahogany legs and a border of tightly grouped nailheads lend formality to a leafy linen print.
5. The Germanic pedestal table in the corner of the living room was greenish in hue; we had it washed in dun gray to make the blue and white *objets* pop. I love the suggestion of artistic creation implied by the Chinese paintbrush. **6.** Large, widely spaced nailheads bring definition to an often-overlooked spot, the stair runner, and also serve an important function of securing the carpet. The lovely flat-weave Elizabeth Eakins rug, also used in the entry, carries the color scheme through the house.

1

2

4

5

3

6

Nailheads and trims are decorative punctuation marks. They add emphasis and communicate eloquently that you've reached the end.

1. We added nailheads to underscore the spherical lines of this wood-and-metal chandelier in the guest room. While a crystal chandelier would have felt out of place, this more rustic version helps fill the volume of space in the cathedral ceiling. **2.** Coordinating but different trims finish a gilded and painted chair in the master bedroom: A multicolored cord outlines the cushions, while a similarly colored gimp finishes the seams where fabric meets frame. **3.** In the kitchen, a box-pleated valance is finished with an airy white beaded trim. The café curtains on the bottom half of the window don't have to match the valance—here they are a simple semi-sheer blue similar to the kitchen chair upholstery. **4.** Woods in a variety of finishes enrich the sunroom. The curved stretchers on the weathered base of this coffee table create a distinctive silhouette. The tabletop is wrapped in leather, with spaced rustic nailheads for another layer of detail. **5.** I find three rows of pillows is generally the "Goldilocks" mean for a well-made bed. However, I have noticed that pillows follow a gender divide. Men: Fewer! Women: More! **6.** Steamer trunks are traditionally trimmed in leather affixed with brass nailheads; here, two sizes of nails, along with the brass hardware, add polish in the guest bedroom.

A FRESH TAKE
ON CLASSICS

A busy young professional couple purchased this duplex apartment with good bones in a prewar city building. They wanted to enhance, not alter, its elegant architecture, but it did need to be updated and cleaned up a bit so that its beauty could shine. Their last apartment had been very monochromatic and neutral; this time they wanted to step out into a bit more color and pattern. While certain rooms, such as the living room and master bedroom, are fairly muted and serene, others, such as the peacock-blue dining room and the husband's sapphire office (seen on pages 4 and 238), up the wattage significantly. In each room there are some elements that speak to the classic architecture

The success of a room is dependent not so much on coordination as on variation—variation in scale, texture, darkness and light, materials, and styles.

and antiques, and other elements that take a more modern and youthful, less formal tone. Thanks to this couple's keen interest in design and their willingness to take risks, we were able to balance classical restraint with vibrant individuality.

When we first walked through the apartment, we all agreed it had beautiful bones and wouldn't need a lot of work, but then we proceeded to alter nearly every surface. Ooops. Some of those changes were an inevitable result of the renovation syndrome: As you fix and perfect one element, everything else suddenly looks a bit shabbier and you see more changes that need to be made. We ended up raising and opening up the double doorways; redoing the baseboards and installing crisper woodwork; repairing the staircase; fixing the chimney flues to eliminate smoky odors; and renovating the kitchen and bathrooms.

The living room is a calming enclave of soft gray greens and taupes enlivened by a few key black and dark wood accents. The mirror makes this room: Its bold-scale geometric frame gives this classic room a bit of zing, as does the Roy Lichtenstein painting (seen on the following pages). We gave the art a strong black frame that connects to the pair of black chests beneath the windows, the sofa table, and the black-framed mirror in the adjacent library. In a room with classic architecture, my first instinct is to approach it as a traditional space. The things you notice most, however, are a result of stepping out of those expectations, as we did with some of the art and the textiles. While this is still a somewhat formal room, we subtly relaxed expectations by choosing wool damask curtains (rather than taffeta, for example); bamboo blinds; a tonal woven wool rug; and quiet plaids and paisleys rather than ornate silks and tassels. The overall effect is understated elegance rather than overt opulence.

PREVIOUS PAGE: In the entrance hall, an antique French *cartonnier* (file cabinet) has elegant leather drawer fronts. A pair of obelisk lamps and the Empire pendant lamp echo the classical elegance of the architecture. OPPOSITE AND FOLLOWING PAGES: Balancing tradition with a more youthful palette, the living room mixes serene pale greens and taupes with accents of black and dark wood for contrast. A clean-lined parchment coffee table is juxtaposed with a softer upholstered ottoman.

We chose two different sofa fabrics—one greenish, one taupe—so we used two different sofa profiles, and added pillows and chairs in paisleys that incorporate both colors. The seating is arranged around the fireplace, which left space behind the sofa for a game table, a wonderful addition to any living space. You can have an intimate meal there, use it as a writing desk, or set it up as a bar when entertaining. In a room of this size, it's always important to vary furniture heights and scale; the card table and console table behind the sofa help achieve that goal. A deeper green-blue leather was used on the game table chairs, with a contrasting zigzag woven on the chairbacks.

Though a library is typically a more traditional room, here it feels lighter and less formal due to the white bookshelves and softer palette. The tufted sofa is in plush linen velvet rather than tobacco leather, and the Charles of London chair, which can often feel masculine due to its straight lines and hefty scale, is upholstered in a printed linen floral stripe, nudging it more toward the feminine.

We raised and enlarged the double doorways with pocket doors, leading to the dining room and the library. Because the doorways create a nice open flow, we wove the color palettes and elements (such as bamboo shades and black frames) throughout the space for a sense of continuity.

OPPOSITE: We redid the bookshelves in the library, adding more detailed moldings to better suit the architecture of the apartment. ABOVE: This is truly a room for reading, not just for watching television, but with the parchment bar cabinet in the corner, it's nice for cozy entertaining as well.

Glossy lacquered walls create a glamorous dining room bathed in shades of cerulean blue. Touches of white in crisp molding, a giltwood chandelier, linen curtains, and the antique rug provide important contrast. The bold color and curvy chairs give the room youthfulness, while the wood furniture and the rug ground it in tradition.

In this apartment, the dining room offers the real "wow!" moment. The color palette intensifies here, and high-gloss lacquered walls create drama. A luminous finish helps counteract the deep hue, which might otherwise have seemed dark or, worse, gloomy. Combined with the artwork, which was found serendipitously after the design, the color bathes the room in rich, aqueous splendor. The crisp white chair rail and moldings, running almost like a racing stripe through the room, bring order and keep the room from veering into the baroque.

We originally considered a red dining room, but given the green tones in the living room, the homeowners chose this vivid peacock blue instead. Sometimes the best thing to do when working within a single color palette is to clash a little. Everything shouldn't be matchy-matchy: Don't be afraid to choose shades that are related but different. The blue of the chairs is different from the blue on the walls, giving the scheme more depth. The tufted seats are upholstered in suede, which is more practical for regular use, while a woven geometric is used on the chair-backs. Printed linen curtains with an ivory ground, white moldings, and the white-and-gold chandelier add lightness.

Touches of blue and coral in the fabrics and furnishings add pop to an all-white
kitchen. While the tile is Carrera marble, the counters are "Super White
Fantasy" quartzite, a natural stone even stronger than granite. The wire-netted
milk-glass lights, inspired by antique factory lighting, are from Remains.

SCROLLS
AND SWIRLS

While many of the fabrics are tone-on-tone or
muted colors, often dressed down on printed linens,
they add an elegant spark to solids and neutrals.
1. Even within the quiet of the master bedroom,
there is pattern: a muted wool paisley (top) from
Cowtan & Tout on the club chair, a faded batik
printed linen from Lee Jofa on curtains, and a waxed
linen stripe from Rogers & Goffigon on the bench.
2. A printed linen paisley from John Rosselli (top)
adds pattern on a pillow in the living room; the
woven carpet from Elizabeth Eakins (right) and
geometric fabric from Claremont, used on the backs
of the card-table chairs, add texture. **3.** The ivory
ground of the floral printed linen from Holland &
Sherry on the dining room curtains provides relief
from the rich blues. A woven geometric from Lee
Jofa adds interest to chairbacks. Using two different
fabrics on chairs is one of my favorite ways to apply
an extra layer of custom detail. **4.** This printed linen
floral stripe from Cowtan & Tout lends subtle
femininity to the Charles of London chair in the
library. **5.** In the family room, a wool plaid from
Clarence House on the club chair, pillows in an
exquisite Fortuny fabric (left), and a woven wool
carpet from Elizabeth Eakins all incorporate shades
of carnelian red. **6.** In the library are a damask
pillow from Carleton V, a leopard-print chenille
from Cowtan & Tout on side chairs, and a camel
linen velvet from Rogers & Goffigon on a pillow.

The chairs and the "metamorphosis" table—so called because an intricate mechanism allows it to open up and expand in diameter with built-in, pie-shaped leaves—are both custom-made. The chairs are slim and tall, and we added low, thin arms onto some of them. It took three prototypes to get the chair exactly right. When you can't find what you want, it's worth the time and effort to have a design custom-made if you can (says the decorator).

The kitchen is a typical urban galley kitchen, but larger. Its wood floors are a wonderful luxury, not only for their appearance, but also for their ease on feet and backs. They do require a little more maintenance over time than stone or tile, however. Carrera marble tile covers the backsplash, and the counters are a bit more unusual—the funnily named but beautiful "Super White Fantasy" quartzite, which is a natural stone (not man-made quartz) that combines the look of marble with the durability of granite. At the homeowners' wise suggestion, we tested a variety of protective finishes, and settled on polishing and sealing the surfaces with a silicone

Gradations of bittersweet orange and brick red in the TV room—
from the linen velvet sofa, to the woven wool rug, to the mini
leopard-print chair—create a color-rich room within a neutral shell.

BATHING IN BEAUTY

Even more than kitchens, baths are utilitarian spaces. It is essential that they feel clean, organized, and (ideally) beautiful, but first and foremost, they must function well. Because the fixtures and materials in a bath are long-lasting and not easily changed, this is not a place to indulge in trends. Kiddie-themed tile borders won't work when your children get older or you sell your house; ditto for pronounced colors and patterns in tiles. I generally like to stick with white (ceramic or marble) for tiles, counters, and fixtures and add color, if desired, with paint (as in the bold blue in the bath off the husband's office, bottom right) or wallpaper (for example, the distinctive lotus pattern from Farrow & Ball in the powder room, top). Similarly, I don't recommend eliminating the bathtub and creating a shower-only bathroom; that can have an impact on resale value because families with young children (not to mention older people and bath lovers of all ages) will always want a tub.

My recommendations and favorites for the bath include:

- Marble basket-weave and herringbone floors. In powder rooms, wood can be a perfect choice.

- Multiple sources of light. The downstairs bath (top left) includes a ceiling fixture, a valance light, and sconces, which can be dimmed for company or turned up for makeup application.

- Large mirrors, which may incorporate a medicine cabinet or, in a powder room, not. Above a dual vanity, a full mirrored wall can be wonderful, with center or side fixed panels for sconces and unobtrusive finger pulls at the bottom for medicine cabinets (as in the master bath, bottom left).

- Towel bars and toilet-paper holders placed after the fixtures have been installed. Rather than spec them on the plans, I prefer to see what works by sight and feel once the bath is finished (as with the towel bar on the wainscot, top right). Sit atop the toilet seat and make sure the TP holder placement is convenient. A towel bar on the shower door can double as a handle (and the towels can serve as a virtual loincloth when you're showering).

- When space is limited, I like chrome train racks (open shelves) installed up high to hold stacks of towels. I put robe hooks on the back of the door, and I prefer double-pronged hooks, which grip better.

- While the trim color is consistent in the rest of the houses I design, I usually make it a brighter white in the bathrooms and kitchens, where the fixtures are whiter. Similarly, if I use brass hardware in the rest of the house, I'll switch to nickel in the bath and do a split finish, with a brass knob on the outside and a nickel one on the bath side of the door (see photo, top right).

- A convex apron atop a flat vanity, which can save space by allowing for a larger sink, with room to stand underneath (top left). If the sink and vanity are both rounded (bottom right), it's a good idea to have furniture feet at the base to make room for human feet, but I normally have a wooden dust panel affixed a few inches behind so the area doesn't become a dirt trap.

sealer to keep stains at bay. Beyond the refrigerator is a little beverage bar, with a coffeemaker and wine fridge—a great way to break up the long expanse of cabinetry and segregate the different workspaces. At the other end is a banquette that originally went even deeper into that corner, which made it hard to get in and out of. We ended up closing off that alcove and putting a coat closet there, and brought the banquette and breakfast table forward, into the natural light. The paneled banquette base has built-in storage, and the table is on locking wheels.

The bedrooms and a family/TV room are upstairs. The TV room is designed for flexibility, so it could easily become a bedroom if needed. We adapted some pieces the couple already owned, reshaping and reviving an *en tableau* chair—the outline of its framed back is visible beneath the upholstery—with a chenille leopard print, and added a linen velvet sofa. The original plan was for the walls to be brick red as well, but we settled on taupe as a more versatile option. Hanging the grid of four architectural prints so that they nearly graze the ceiling seemed counterintuitive at first, but it makes the ceiling feel higher. On the opposite wall, a row of three classical prints incorporates the TV in their composition.

The master bedroom is as serene as a bedroom should be, purposely kept spare, monochromatic, and tailored. Windows on two walls provide a romantic view of the tops of brownstones that evoke Paris. We lowered the ceiling slightly to add a layer of soundproofing for sound sleeping. Monochromatic fabrics keep the palette hushed as well. The heavily lined curtains, blackout Roman shades, and wall-to-wall carpet further enhance the quietude. Slender night tables were custom-made to fit the narrow spaces beside the bed.

Our aim was to create interiors that would be neither so novel or trendy, nor so traditional or predictable, that the couple would tire of them. Finding that balance and elegant simplicity is, I suppose, the ultimate goal of every project.

OPPOSITE: Silver heirlooms add a cool gleam. ABOVE: In the enveloping calm of the pale gray and blue bedroom (painted Farrow & Ball "Light Blue," one of my favorites), white linens, moldings, and the mantel add clarity. Intaglios framed in black above the fireplace are the inverse of the white mantel framing the black firebox.

SUBTLE TOUCHES OF PATTERN

Pattern is used judiciously to give rooms impact and interest without overwhelming the eye. **1.** The antique rug and the curtain fabric needed pattern to balance the solid fields of the lacquered walls and large table in the dining room. This expandable metamorphosis table was custom-made for us with a classical Biedermeier-style base and Regency top. **2.** The wide octagonal frame of the antiqued mirror in the living room is subtly echoed in the petaled medallion of the marble mantel. **3.** A Chinese porcelain platter on the lacquered linen coffee table in the library nicely ties together the colors of the room. I like to have a big dish or platter and a stack of books on a coffee table; the round element helps break up the linearity. **4.** The ebonized legs of the Napoleon III chair in the living room contrast with all the skirted pieces that surround it. Great chair frames like this can often be found at antique shows, and with reupholstering, they are usually every bit as good as new furniture. A paisley pillow adds a bit of exotic flair to the windowpane plaid chair. **5.** I have long coveted this *cartonnier*, so it was a delight to place it here, where I can come visit it. The beautiful tooled leather fronts open to reveal file drawers. **6.** The dark, ebonized Napoleon III table behind the living room sofa has a flip top that doubles it in size. Ceramic garden stools beneath the table add pattern as well as extra seating in a pinch.

2

3

5

6

1

2

4

5

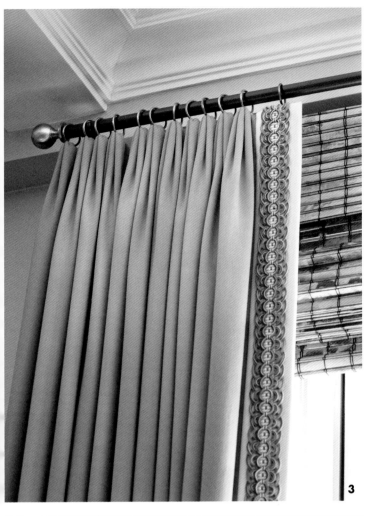

3

6

Tiles, nailheads, trims, piping, and pleats create a layer of subtle geometry that animates a room.

1. In the wife's home office, a shaped valance, underscored with pleats and a tassel fringe, offers elegant polish to a Roman shade made with a beautiful embroidered medallion fabric. While an office might not seem an obvious place for such special window treatments, they elevate the whole room. **2.** A grooved ceramic lamp in luminous cognac, from Christopher Spitzmiller; pillows in a Fortuny pattern and silk stripe; and multitone cording on the velvet sofa infuse layers of lushness into the family/TV room. **3.** In the library, an ornate braid is applied to a contrasting cuff on the curtains to give it more prominence. The curtain poles mix bronze with brass finials. **4.** Ropelike trim edges bright coral paisley pillows in the kitchen; the same fabric is used on the shade of the pendant lamp over the banquette. The blue-and-white herringbone cushions are edged in coordinating orange piping. Carrera marble tiles introduce geometry of a different scale. **5.** At a round dining table, chairs don't typically have arms, but the owners requested them on four of the chairs, so we designed low, thin ones with curved supports that could slide beneath the table. Brass nailheads finish the seat. **6.** The top back corners of the Charles of London chair in the library are outlined with antiqued brass nailheads for a distinctive detail.

THE DETAILS

They say the devil is in the details, and it's true, but so is all that is divine. It's not only the custom finishing touches that distinguish a beautifully designed room from the mass-produced norm; it's also the attention to detail from the very beginning: understanding why one sofa silhouette will work better than another, or how to balance the mix of skirted and wood-frame upholstery in a room, or how to judge the quality of workmanship in window treatments.

In this section, I want to pull back the curtain, so to speak, and reveal some of the nitty-gritty, nuts-and-bolts insider info that guides the literally hundreds, if not thousands, of choices we make with homeowners on every project. As they appeared in my "Where To" column for the *Wall Street Journal*, here, printed together, are some of my most pressing thoughts on how high to hang curtains, sconces, or a chair rail; how much floor to show around an area rug; or how to arrange artwork.

SHARPIE DRAWINGS

My secret weapon began when I worked on a grand "cottage" in New Orleans. I have always drawn floor plans, perspective sketches, and elevations (vertical views of each wall and its furnishings) for projects, but I had never used photographs in the process before. These homeowners already had some furnishings in place, and I was trying to diagnose where the problems were and show how I wanted to solve them. The couple was about to toss everything and begin anew, but I thought their frustrations were getting the better of them. So I took photos of their existing rooms and started sketching in, with a Sharpie marker, what I thought we should add or eliminate, and where. In some cases, I would just draw right over pieces I didn't like, substituting my recommendations; in others, I would draw in my fantasies of the ideal pieces of furniture or artwork to complete a room.

Not only did it help my clients more clearly envision the finished room, but it also aided me in my design process. Whereas with a photograph, the scale, proportion, and room details are more or less accurate, when I am just sketching freehand my drawings aren't always to scale. I might draw furniture a little larger to overcompensate for clients who always want to fit in more, or I might design curtains without remembering to account for a soffit above the windows. Sharpie drawings also helped me communicate more clearly with tradespeople and collaborators—staff at the curtain workroom could clearly see the proportions I had in mind and where we planned to hang the curtains, and measure accordingly. Even better, they could see where I ultimately wanted to end up, and could troubleshoot to help me get there.

Then a funny thing started to happen: It was kind of like a decorating version of *The Secret*. When I drew things from my imagination that I thought would be ideal for the space—even something as specific as an antique or an accessory—I would find it in real life. My first Sharpie client became a Sharpie addict, and I had to explain that just because I drew a round cartouche hanging above the bed didn't mean we would end up finding that exact thing as it existed in my mind. Now I use Sharpie drawings on nearly every project, whether it's from-scratch construction or an existing room we're editing. You can see how it works on the next pages.

BEFORE,
SHARPIE,
AND AFTER

STEP 1: Photograph the existing space. **STEP 2:** Draw in
the desired furniture, window treatments, and even
accessories. **STEP 3:** Turn it into reality.

FIRST ROW, FROM LEFT TO RIGHT: In the family house in
Connecticut seen in the second chapter, the homeowners were ready to add some finishing pieces. For
more contrast with the light walls and rug, in place of
the painted breakfront I drew a black Napoleon III
bookcase, which we then found. We added curtains
flanking the French doors and changed the sofa table
from a drop-leaf to a clean-lined parchment Parsons
table. I drew in the staircase model as an example of an
accessory, and we were actually able to find one. SECOND
ROW: The owners were renovating the city apartment in
the fourth chapter from scratch. We had created the
plan, were in construction, and were ready to choose
the furniture. I drew in a three-dimensional scheme on
the photo, including lamps, artwork sizes, and window
treatments. It helped the clients understand how much
space the back-to-back sofas would take up. Drawing
the curtains helped me realize the poles were long
enough that I might need to plan for center brackets.
THIRD ROW: In the blue-and-white house in Florida in
the third chapter, which was new construction, I learned
not to draw in anything too esoteric, because the owner
then wanted us to find those exact items. This project
was designed entirely by Sharpie, and with few exceptions, the finished rooms look just like the drawings.

CURTAINS:
A PRIMER

From adding softness, color, and pattern, to muffling sound and providing warmth, curtains contribute so much that a room often feels naked without them. Whenever homeowners ask me where *not* to skimp when it comes to decorating, I always say, "Curtains!" While different tiers of furniture quality can be tolerated and, frankly, offer welcome financial relief, it's worth investing in curtains that are masterfully crafted, whenever possible.

One of the first decisions when choosing curtains is whether you want to see the pole or curtain rod. When curtains hang on a pole from rings, the hardware is visible, and decorative; when they hang on a track from hooks or clips, the hardware and track are hidden. A track is not as decorative, but the curtains move back and forth easily. This is important in a bedroom, for example, where you may be opening and closing them frequently. One solution that offers the best of both worlds: a slotted pole with a concealed track. The curtains hang on J-hooks that slip into the bottom of the pole. Rings on a wooden pole can be noisy, and because of the space between the curtain and the pole, they don't block the light quite as well as curtains on a track, but I do like poles and rings in less formal or more modern rooms.

In bedrooms, I typically use curtains that are held in place on a track, with blackout shades beneath them for total light control. A valance neatly finishes the top of the window treatment and also conceals the track and shades. I love the polished look of valances, and all the decorative possibilities they offer. I line all my curtains with blackout material, so the curtains are weightier and block light better and the fabric is preserved from fading.

For curtains in other rooms, I still use a basic lining, blackout lining, and interlining for fullness, but sometimes I add an extra "bump," or a layer of felt, for even more gravitas. Silk curtains must be properly lined; otherwise sunlight will rot them. The only time I don't use lining is with sheers or gauzy fabrics. In a house, where the windows will be seen from the outside, I line all the curtains with what's called a "fancy" lining, usually with a small arabesque pattern, which looks much prettier from outside than plain muslin. It also lends the house a nice uniformity.

I like to trim curtains along the leading and bottom edges only. From a practical standpoint, those are the two edges that typically get the most wear; trimming these also looks the prettiest. (Trim placed along the top of the curtain appears to truncate its height.) I put the trim right along the edge, not inset, so that it will protect and reinforce the edges. If the curtains are simple, or more tailored, I add ¼-inch contrast trim for a crisp finish. My preference is for curtains to break ½ inch to 1 inch on the floor, like a trouser hem. I'm not one for puddling, which looks sloppy to me.

WHERE TO HANG CURTAINS

There is a reason movie gangsters always threaten that "it'll be curtains" for those who cross them: Curtains can be deadly, difficult, and quite literally a drag. It's hard to know where to hang them; the best placement can vary greatly depending on the room, the style of curtains, and architecture.

First things first: Curtains are a powerful tool in a decorator's arsenal. In addition to contributing softness and discreet pattern (since heavy patterning is, in part, shadowed within folds), they can and should add height by virtue of their verticality. Curtain panels, at their most basic level, are two swaths of fabric bracketing a window. I ardently dislike when they hug the top of the window casing in such a way as to truncate the window and the view (FIGURE A). For this reason, I like to place them up high, close to or just underneath a room's crown molding (FIGURE B). This makes the window appear taller (and as a bonus, can help hide the appearance of the pole). As much as I would love to espouse this as an unbreakable rule, though, it isn't that simple.

When the space between a window's casing (the trim around the window) and the crown molding is expansive, I split the difference between the window casing and the crown, and hang the pole in the middle (FIGURE C). This offers some lift (and goodness knows, I'm always looking for a bit of that), without highlighting a big chunk of empty wall.

It is just as important to be mindful of where curtains hit at the sides. Nobody likes obscuring a window, so whenever possible, it's best if the curtains cover more wall to the left and right of the window than window glass. They should also cover the window casing. Given that curtains generally stack in the 8-inch to 10-inch range (the amount of space they take up when drawn open completely), check to be sure there is enough wall next to the window in question. Many windows are placed near corners, so this is an important consideration. If wall space is tight, you may need to opt for lighter-weight fabrics that don't take up as much space or a different solution such as a Roman shade; or live with the curtains covering more of the glass.

Finally, a small pet peeve: I know others disagree, but I prefer to call them curtains, not draperies or drapes.

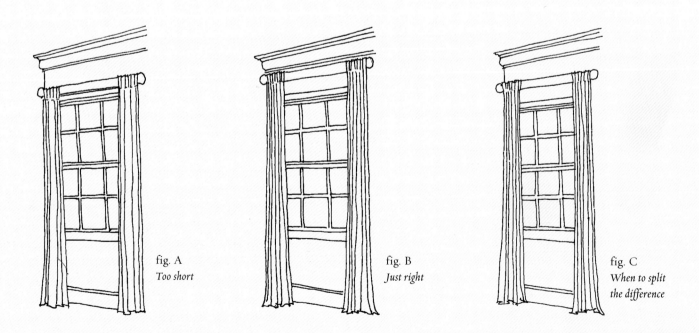

fig. A
Too short

fig. B
Just right

fig. C
When to split the difference

CURTAIN HEADINGS

Not all pleats are created equal: The type of pleat, or curtain heading, you choose creates different looks and levels of formality. It's important to look not only at the pleat itself, but at how it affects the fabric beneath it. I like to vary curtain headings from room to room to add interest.

1. Cartridge pleat: This has distinct loops of fabric, as if each pleat were molded around a cartridge. It is very linear, creating almost a striped effect. This works best with a fabric with some body to it; it can look modern or traditional depending on the material. **2.** Shirred pleat: The fullness of this heading adds volume and dimension to a fabric. Pleats such as this, which create a pronounced vertical column, don't work as well with stripes, which are not likely to line up precisely along the pleat. **3.** Pinch pleat (three pleats): This pretty pleat is gathered only at the top, so it has a softness to it. It works well with café curtains and other simple window treatments. **4.** French pleat (three pleats): French pleats are gathered a bit below the top of the curtain, creating a slight fan above the gather. They are an elegant, traditional heading that works well in a variety of settings. **5.** Pinch pleat (two pleats): This pleat is gathered at the top to create a more vertical, linear effect than a triple or French pleat. **6.** French pleat (two pleats): French pleats don't work well with bulky or thick fabrics. They are perfect for silks, lightweight wool challis, and other fabrics suited to its delicate folds. **7.** Butterfly pleat: This is one of my favorite and most frequently used headings. These pleats are hand-detailed but also substantial. The softly rounded top has pleasing proportions. **8.** Goblet pleat: This distinctive pleat is more structural and noticeable; it's the curtain equivalent of adding crown molding to a room. It's not for delicate, floating fabrics, though. **9.** Inverted pleat (or reverse box pleat): This pleat is stitched down flat from the top, for perfect modern simplicity.

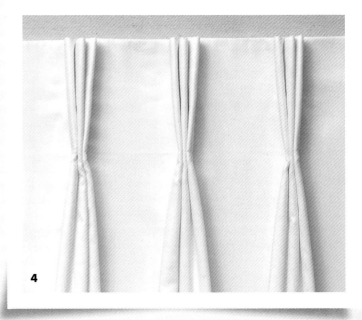

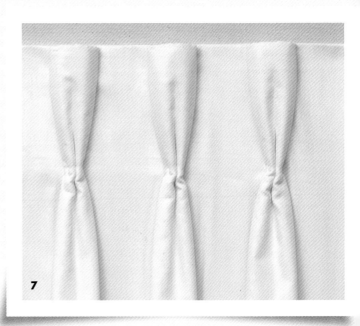

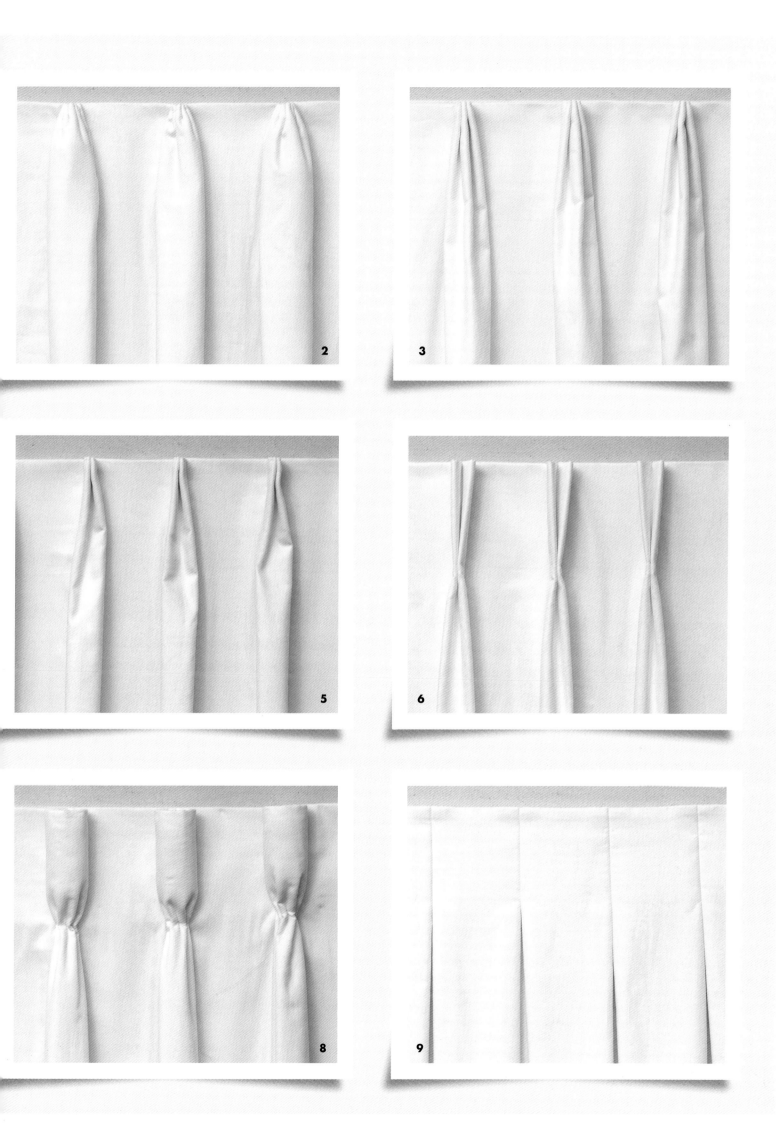

VALANCES AND SWAGS

Valances add a polished finish and are especially helpful for concealing shades or blinds—in a bedroom, for example. Along with Roman and balloon shades, and swags, valances work when there isn't room for curtain panels to extend to the floor—for example, in a kitchen or bath, or over a radiator cover. In the room above, the swags finish the windows without blocking the glorious view. These are swags with bells, which are the pleats that curve out between each swag. **1.** A box-pleat valance is a nice tailored option for concealing a roller shade. We used a deeper one in the Florida living room on page 74. **2.** Balloon shades can be blackout-lined for bedrooms. They are pretty in girls'

rooms. (I prefer Roman shades in boys' bedrooms, so the children don't try to swing from the curtains.) **3.** This is a waterfall balloon shade with a gathered heading and tails, which makes it fancier. **4.** *En tableau* curtains have strings sewn in to pull them back as if they were stage curtains. The strings hold them back at a higher point than simple tiebacks would, which offsets the fact that *en tableau* curtains cover more window at the top. **5.** A swag and jabot, with cascading tails, was a hallmark of the 1980s. I use them less frequently now, but I chose them for my own bedroom when a radiator cover precluded full curtain panels, and they dressed the windows beautifully.

1

2

3

4

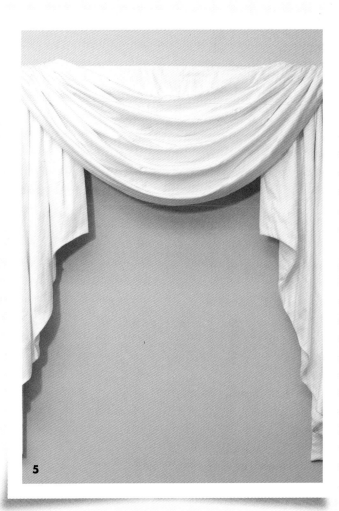

5

UPHOLSTERY:
A PRIMER

To the uninitiated, upholstered chairs and sofas may all appear the same, but in fact, they are alike only in the way that, say, all cars are alike. The silhouette, size and scale, the pitch of the back and style of arm, the types of cushion and stuffing, and many other details contribute to each piece's individual style, comfort level, and suitability for a particular space. Just as you would never buy a car without test-driving it, it is incredibly helpful to try sitting and even lounging in a chair or sofa before buying it. For example, I love to sit cross-legged; therefore, a T-cushion seat, where the cushion extends and wraps around the arms, gives me room to spread out. A beefy guy or petite woman can feel alternately squished or swallowed up in chairs that aren't sized well for them. And it's not simply a person's height; it's also the proportions: Are you long-legged or short-waisted? The depth of the seat or the height of the back is going to make a difference.

SOME GENERALITIES:

- Loose backs, which have a separate back cushion, aren't going to look as tailored as tight backs (where there is no cushion), but they are going to feel softer and more comfortable, so I often use them in bedrooms. (Of course, you can always add a lumbar or throw pillow to soften a tight back.)

- A tight back will require less fabric to upholster, while a loose back and a skirted chair will require more. More fabric invariably means more expense.

- I always like to have a mix of skirted and unskirted (that is, with exposed wooden legs, or what's called a "show wood" base) pieces and a mix of different silhouettes (scroll backs, rounded tub chairs, square backs, tufted backs, turned legs, straight legs, etc.) in a room. It's important to vary the visual rhythm of furniture. On the other hand, pairs of chairs also lend nice symmetry to a room; in this case, both members of the pair should be treated the same. In my office, changing fabrics or trims on a matching pair just for variety is a big no-no.

- If you will be seeing a sofa or chair from the back, a scroll back is more attractive than a big, blocky square back.

- How you have the cushions stuffed is a personal preference. A foam core wrapped in down holds its shape better, but 100 percent down feels softer. However, you must be willing to commit to frequent fluffing, because that's how down gets its bounce back; otherwise it will "pancake."

MY FAVORITE CHAIR SILHOUETTES

1. A "show wood" base with dark wooden legs, tailored lines, and nailheads give this chair a more masculine feel. It's similar to a Jansen chair, except the Jansen usually has spiraling turned legs. The tight back resembles an *en tableau* back, where the cushioning is framed and raised. Here it is outlined by nailheads. **2.** Perhaps because of its curves, the Paley chair feels a little more feminine to me than the typical club chair. It has a pitched, scrolled back, with Lawson, or rolled, arms. **3.** While tufted sofas and chairs are often thought of in connection with libraries, they are appropriate for any room. The Abbott chair's straight back contrasts with curved Napoleon III arms emphasized by pleating.

4. There is almost nowhere you couldn't place the classic Bridgewater—it is equally at home in both living rooms and bedrooms. Here, the dressmaker, or waterfall, skirt, which falls flat, unseamed, from the base of the seat, gives the chair a more modern feel. This chair has a loose back and a T-seat cushion, which wraps around the saddle arm.

5. I find the Odom chair to be as versatile as the Bridgewater. This silhouette, with its rounded seat cushion (a modified T-cushion), and Lawson arm, is a little more feminine, and well suited to smaller spaces such as bedrooms, but it works equally well, larger scale, in public rooms.

6. Like the Abbott above it, the Marsha chair is a handsome alternative to a club chair. With its scrolled back and arms, it creates a nice silhouette from any angle. It's wide enough to curl up in, but it does sit low to the ground, which can make it harder for an older person to stand up from it.

7

8

10

11

It is smartest to "try before you buy." Everyone is proportioned differently, so what's comfortable for one person may not be for another.

7. This split-back, scroll-back chair is similar to a Napoleon III–style chair. The chair has a tight seat as well as a tight back, which means it's firmer and less fluffy, but it also has a fuss-free, clean-lined silhouette. The turned front legs and straight back legs on casters give it portability. **8.** This is a loose-back variation on the Paley chair shown on the previous spread (#2). It has wooden legs rather than a skirted base, and while it has the characteristic angled seat back, here the back is straight rather than scrolled. The curving base contributes to the angled feel. Pitched, set-back arms have flat-faced, welted fronts. **9.** The Charles of London chair has a tailored silhouette that is perfect for libraries and more masculine settings, but it's also very comfortable. It is distinguished by its low, flat arms, shield back, broad T-cushion, and square, simple base. It can be skirted (as seen in the library, page 198), or have wooden feet, as seen here. I prefer straight legs to the bun feet that are traditionally used with this chair style. **10.** The tub chair is another classic. It has a curved back that slopes down with just a small curve to form arms. Tub chairs make ideal bedroom chairs. Or, since they are not overly large or heavy, they can be placed on a swivel base so they can turn for TV-watching or conversation. **11.** The tub chair's curved, concave back offers a pleasing contrast to square-back chairs. It's smaller-scaled and more sheltering than a club chair. This tub chair variation has Lawson arms and a split back. **12.** With a tufted back and sloped arms, this tub chair is known as a Marshall Field chair.

FRAME CHAIRS

Wooden frame chairs with open arms give airy relief
to a room filled with upholstered sofas and chairs.
1. A curvaceous Venetian chair is a flight of fancy
compared with most traditional silhouettes. It's like a
piece of sculpture, just exotic enough to stand out
without going over the top. **2.** This Louis XIV straight-
back, upright chair is more formal in feeling than the
oval-back chair below it. **3.** The Louis XVI chair has
a curved back and a cushioned seat that make it more
comfortable as a dining chair. I like the custom of
putting a different fabric on the chairbacks, since they
have a defined space that works well for this.
4. Bergères are frame chairs that have upholstered,
closed arms. Here, the sides of the sculptural scrolled
arms are caned, which makes the chair a little different
from a traditional bergère.

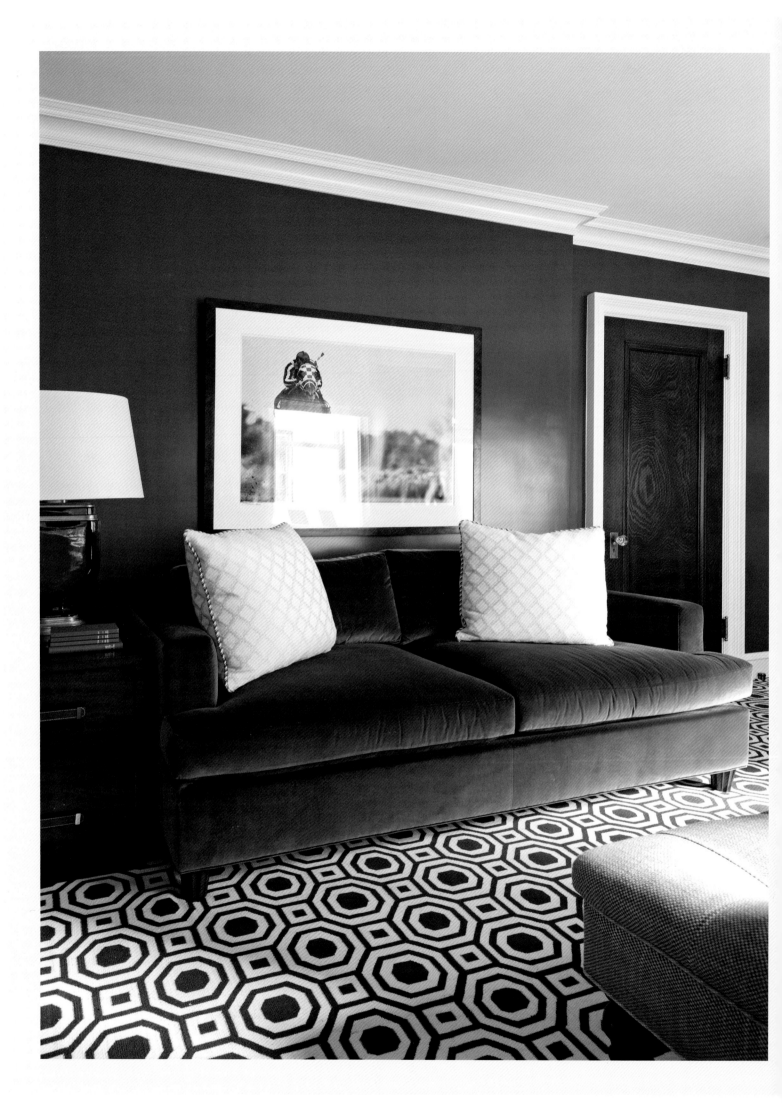

The Lawson sofa (here and opposite) has a low, square, tight back, and arms (whether square or rolled) that are lower than the back. If left unskirted, it feels modern, linear, and a touch more masculine; skirted, with piping and pillows, it's at home in more traditional rooms.

Tufting adds geometric interest to upholstery. This sofa has the comfort of low, rolled arms and the support of a high back; if the arms were the same height as the back, this would be closer to the traditional shape of a Chesterfield sofa, that classic of men's clubs and libraries.

The St. Thomas sofa is what I grew up with. It is the most comfortable sofa on earth, because you can lie down on it like a daybed. The sheltering arms and back are the same height. In all black in the 1970s, this sofa was sleek and super cool; in the '80s, my father recovered it in green fabric with off-white piping in a roomful of chintz for a totally traditional transformation.

The Carr sofa is the big daddy of all poufy sofas. It's the perfect shape if you want curves and comfort. Its generous rolled arms make it cozy for napping (an important consideration, in my opinion), and a gently curved, tight back softens its lines. This sofa also works well tufted.

My father always referred to this as a Horseguard sofa; therefore, so do I. It has a classic shape, with an upright back but comfortable, loose cushions and the tidy scroll of a Lawson arm. Without T-cushions on the seat, it looks orderly and symmetrical.

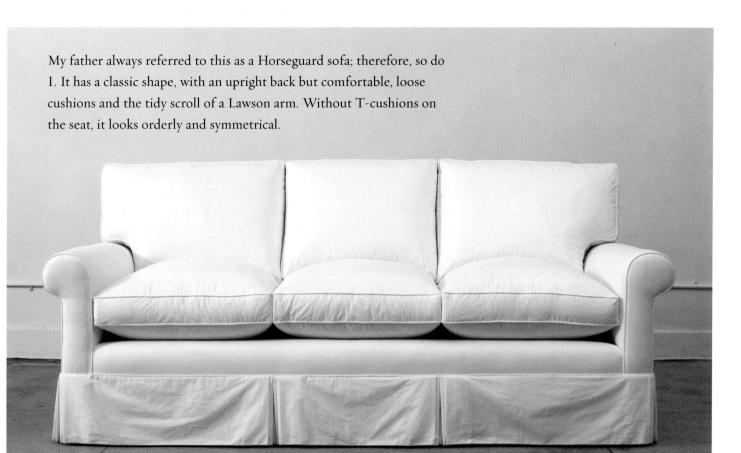

The Bridgewater is to sofas what steak is to food. It is one of my go-to sofas, and often works as a building block in a room. This is sort of the Platonic ideal of a sofa, with loose seat cushions, a nice saddle arm, and a tight, scrolled back that always looks neat from the front and nice from behind.

WHERE TO PLACE CHAIR RAILS

The placement of chair rails is frequently misunderstood in modern design, and not just by homeowners, but also by contractors and even some designers. A chair rail is meant to cap the top of a room's dado, or wainscoting, and to keep a chair's back from scraping the wall (FIGURE A). Admittedly, there is no epidemic of chairs scraping walls to drive our interest in chair rail placement. At this point, chair rails are like a room's appendix—nice to have, but largely vestigial. Nonetheless, they function visually to create scale in a room. They have a relatively elementary, unchanging relationship to the ground. I like my chair rails in the range of 28 inches to 30 inches off the finished floor. This is high enough to catch a chair's back, no matter its pitch, but not so tall as to visually swallow up a dining table (typically 29 inches high).

Everywhere I look, though, I see chair rails creeping up the wall. As ceiling heights have become more august in newly constructed houses, many people seem to feel they must raise the height of the chair rails to be proportionate (FIGURE B). This couldn't be more wrong. The chair rail is not the waist of the room, nor is it a belt, whose placement changes with the height of the person wearing it. The chair rail is about that chair—and chair seat and back heights just don't change that much, even when they are scaled up. When chair rails are placed high up off the floor, these great, tall rooms look just like their shorter counterparts, and lose a lot of the sex appeal of being taller in the first place. Instead, at the standard, appropriate height, when combined with tall ceilings, they will emphasize the sweep of a room (FIGURE C).

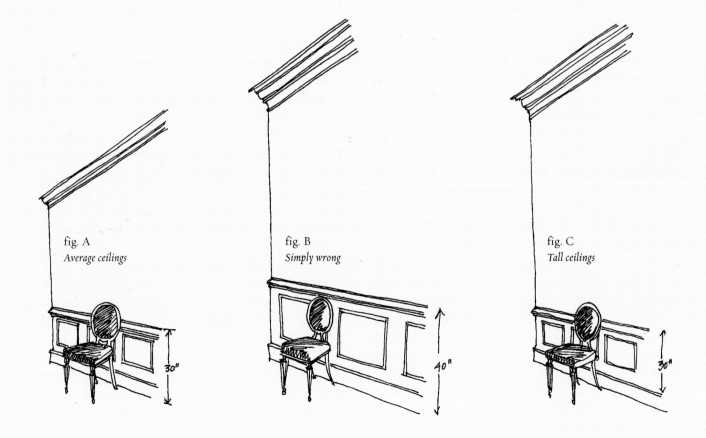

fig. A
Average ceilings

fig. B
Simply wrong

fig. C
Tall ceilings

WHERE FOR ART THOU?

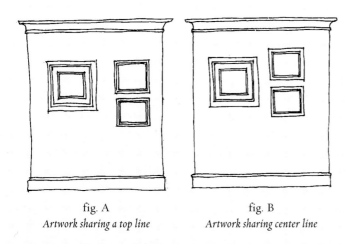

fig. A
Artwork sharing a top line

fig. B
Artwork sharing center line

Art: beautiful to look at, but tricky to hang. Determining where to hang art is much easier when you remember one important thing: It is meant to be seen. So, to a certain extent, there is an intuitive aspect to picture hanging. Don't let your art hang way, way up by the ceiling, and don't let it hug the floor, unless you are extremely tall or extremely short, in which case, you are entirely justified in your acute choices.

I choose to take an average approach when hanging art. As a woman who is 5 feet 9 inches tall, I feel I represent the masses. The national average for American women is 5 feet 4 inches (or 64 inches), and the average American male is 5 feet 9½ inches (or 69½ inches), so I am right in the thick of things. As a result, I usually pick 64 inches to 66 inches off the floor as the center point (not hanging height) for artwork, as it can suit many heights.

When I hang clusters of art, I mass them on that same center point. When stacking artwork, I never line up paintings to share a top or bottom line (FIGURE A). Instead, I arrange them to share a center line (FIGURE B). Much as when one draws in perspective, and there is a single vanishing point to determine the whole composition, an arrangement of pictures, when organized around a single center line, or point, will successfully hang together as a whole.

By the same token, artwork that hangs over a piece of furniture—be it a sofa or a table—should be close enough that it relates to the piece as part of a whole composition (FIGURE C). To achieve this, it can be released from the 64-inch directive. If it is too high from the furniture that should anchor it, it will look like it has drifted off into outer space (FIGURE D).

The last important thing to remember: If you are hanging a painting over a sofa or a chair, make sure it is high enough that your head won't hit it when you are seated. Nothing looks good if you're nursing a concussion.

fig. C
Part of a composition

fig. D
Off in limbo

HIGH LIGHTS:
WHERE TO HANG SCONCES

Light is a mysterious thing. It can have a profound effect on a space. It can make an interior cozy or unwelcoming. By illuminating a path, it can subliminally direct traffic. Light can make a room's inhabitants look more, or less, appealing. It can show dirt or hide it. The best way to tackle lighting, therefore, is by first identifying what you want from it.

Obviously, light should primarily allow a person to see. I have been told by lighting designers that the most successful and pleasing way to light a room is to have illumination from all the traditional sources, and at varying degrees, all at once: ambient and overhead, from table lamps and sconces. I love ambient light, such as bookcase lights, because they can expand our sense of a room's size, but you cannot really read by them. I dislike overheads as a rule because they create ugly shadows, but they are tremendously useful when something has gone missing. Table lamps cast wonderful, warm light, but outlets are often available only around a room's perimeter, which can plunge a room's center into darkness. Therefore, I think sconces can offer some of the best, most useful overall lighting for a room, but they can also be the hardest to position.

A standard height for the placement of the bulb (not the sconce's back plate) is 68 inches off the floor. The most important thing to remember is that the sconce should not be so high that you can see the lightbulb under the shade when passing close by. Not only is this view unattractive, but it will also blow out your eyesight. Likewise, if the light is placed too low, it can cast ghoulish shadows on a person's face.

There is one important exception to this height directive: On a staircase wall, you want a sconce to be high enough overhead that you do not accidentally bump into it when descending. So when your electrician is preparing to hang a sconce in your stairwell, always check it first in person before it's wired into place.

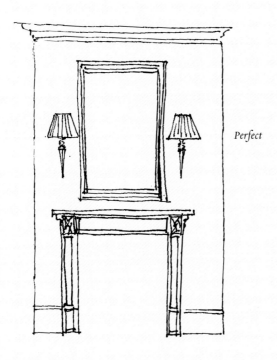

Perfect

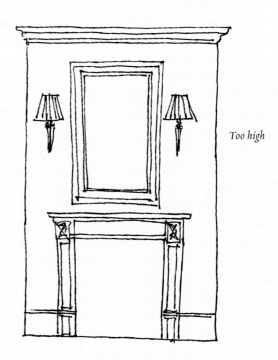

Too high

THE NUTS AND BOLTS
OF HARDWARE

Hardware is the jewelry of a room, the twinkle that speaks to our magpie brains, the scintillating gleam of metal that, done right, adds the final polish. It should not be an afterthought, but rather an integral part of the architectural and design decision-making process. There is hardware that is so sculptural and beautiful it makes a room feel elegant even before the furniture has arrived. I'm thinking of the wonderful cremone bolts on casement windows and French doors in old European houses, the solid brass knobs worn by centuries of hands, the intricate escutcheons that make a front door feel ceremonial and solid. While modern-day hardware may not be quite as elaborate, there are many handsome, well-made options with a very fine level of detail from which to choose.

- The first consideration for a knob or handle should be how it feels in your hand. It should be both comfortable and solid. I am partial to egg-shaped knobs (1), which are clean-lined and elegant. If you have a big hand, a standard cup pull (2) may squish your fingers, and you may need to choose a larger version (they can be custom-sized) or a handle instead.

- My favorite knobs are unlacquered brass, which develops a warm patina from the natural oils on people's hands. If it gets too dark, it can be polished, but I never feel the need to.

- I tend to use knobs more than lever-type handles (3 and 4), which can droop drunkenly when they're not tightened properly, but on French doors, lever handles can be very attractive and are an appropriate choice, both functionally and aesthetically.

- In a kitchen, I often opt for knobs on upper cabinet doors, pulls on drawers, and latches on under-counter doors. Having a "system" such as this gives a sense of order and repetition, and offers a subtle, psychological key to what's what. In a smaller kitchen, I will keep hardware more uniform; but in a larger kitchen, variety helps relieve the monotony of long banks of cabinetry.

- As a rule of thumb, I like knobs to be no less than 1¼ inches in diameter. On paneled, frame cabinet doors with a stile (vertical molding) and rail (horizontal molding), the knob should be placed so the top part of the rail bisects the center of the knob; it should not be placed in the center of the rail. If the knob is placed too low, the door will bow, and if it is too high, it will be uncomfortable to use.

- Chrome has a bluer cast; nickel is warmer, which is why I generally prefer it when a silver hue is called for. Crystal knobs are lovely for bathrooms.

- If there are built-ins throughout the house, I will generally choose a single knob type to use for all of them, with the exception of the kitchen and bath. Built-in cabinetry and bookcases often benefit from an edge detail or a slightly fancier knob.

- Not all metals have to match. For example, curtain rods or metal-edged tables may have brass hardware or accents while the room hardware is nickel. The more you mix metals, the less any one finish will stand out.

- Even hinges can be beautiful, such as the oiled bronze one with raised knuckles called out in brass (5), and one with a round finial (6). The oval pull (7) is designed to be recessed into pocket doors.

HOW BIG AN AREA RUG?

What covers the floor of a room is a central part (quite literally) of one's experience of that space. Marble floors can feel grand and imposing; wood floors, stately; tiled floors, bathroom-y. Rugs also exert influence on the rooms in which they are placed. They protect the floors, they muffle sound, and they lend softness to the hardscape, as it were. In New York City, we are often even required by building regulations to cover up to 80 percent of our floors with rugs or carpeting. Despite area rugs' ubiquity, though, many people find sizing them confusing. As with everything else, I believe there is an intuitive method to finding the right size rug for a room.

As a rule, I choose a regular shape: a rectangle or square. Round rugs always make me think of bath mats. In rooms with attractive floors, I prefer area rugs that show some of the surface they are covering. In truly big rooms, this means that I tend to leave a foot (and sometimes up to 18 inches) of floor exposed around the perimeter. If the room's floors have their own border (such as inlaid wood), I try to keep it visible. However, I am always leery of leaving too big a space around rugs. The result is that the rug appears to be a postage stamp floating on the floor. In smaller rooms, I reduce the border of exposed floor to 6 to 12 inches. The biggest determining factor for sizing a rug is where the walkways in the room will be. You must either cover the walkways or not. You cannot bisect a walkway, because people are more likely to trip where the rug ends.

It is also important to have some of the furniture half on and half off the rug. Big pieces of furniture at a room's edge, such as a sofa or a large club chair or a console table, are perfect for this half-on, half-off approach. It ties together all the room's elements (and most rugs are not so thick that you have to worry about the furniture tilting). The exception to this principle is dining rooms. Here, the rug must extend well past the chairs at the table, to allow them to be moved in and out easily when people sit down or get up.

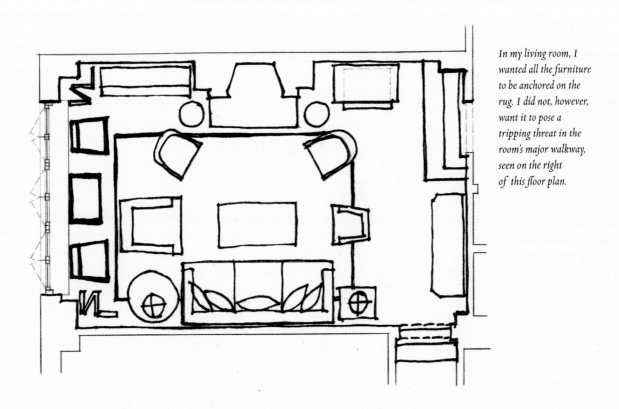

In my living room, I wanted all the furniture to be anchored on the rug. I did not, however, want it to pose a tripping threat in the room's major walkway, seen on the right of this floor plan.

ACKNOWLEDGMENTS

As always, I have a large debt of gratitude for all of the help, support, and guidance that by necessity go into producing any book. William Clark, my agent, is the reason I am producing books and not watching even more television than I already do. So, I think I should thank him, but then I think: wait a minute, why aren't I watching more TV?! Maybe my husband should thank him. After all, I suppose William is the reason I no longer sing advertising jingles to my children in lieu of lullabies (well, William and the makers of the DVR).

At my publisher, Potter Style, I am entirely grateful to Aliza Fogelson, my editor extraordinaire, who is a seriously smart cookie with great advice and vision who looks as if she is only fifteen. Jane Treuhaft is another vital member of our team, providing art direction and thoughtful, philosophical guidance. I always know that if she is telling me something, it is considered and earnest and that I should listen. Finally, I am thankful to Doris Cooper, who allows me to produce these books and is encouraging and fun and only ever supportive. A million thanks to the other vital members of my wonderful Potter team: Kim Tyner, Terry Deal, Pam Krauss, Jim Massey, Emma Brodie, and Jenna Dolan.

The amazing Jill Simpson is the reason the book has full sentences, punctuation, sense, and style. I can't imagine writing a book without her, and the writing is just a tiny part of her vital contribution. I thank her, and I thank heavens. She also introduced me to the wickedly talented Doug Turshen, who designed this book. Doug has literally produced every single design book I have admired in recent and in not-so-recent years. To have Doug as our secret weapon was thrilling, and his wonderful colleague Steve Turner was also a kind and efficient joy with whom to work.

Two legendary photographers who contributed to this book are the incomparable Scott Frances and Durston Saylor. Scott did most of the photography in my first book, and he is magnificent and a dear friend. Durston, another titan, is also a wonderful photographer and friend. I am extremely grateful to them both.

Steve Freihon is this book's principal photographer, magic man, and heart and soul. He produced all the vignettes in the last book and most of the photography in this book. He also got married to a beautiful woman and had a beautiful baby in this period, so I am lucky he found the time to do this different labor of love. Thank you, Natalie and Bowie, for sparing him.

Special thanks to my wonderful clients: Rosana, Liz, and Chris; Linda and Gordon; Sandy and Brian; Gordon and Holt; Greg and Michelle; and Kate and Scott. These are some of the most stylish people I know, all of whom have such an understanding of design, either learned, innate, or both. We all felt honored to work with you, because, like the best of houses, the ones featured here truly were the product of a collaboration with you.

Last but not least, my unparalleled colleagues give their talent, their professionalism, their time, and their fun to all of our projects. I am so incredibly grateful to be in an office with a group of amazing, funny people. They are Dip-Min Yuen, Mee Pinheiro, Pat O'Brien, Kate Callahan, Devon Morten, Lucinda Sussman, Sara Mullen, LeeLee Duryea, Hannah Smith, Bobby Rivera, and Tigran Guylan.

I adore and am grateful to my family. Thank you to Pavlos, Michalis, Markos, Aliki, Duane, Kate, Aunt Paula, Celia, Josefa, Denise, Aunt Rachel, Betsy, Mark, Robin, Emily, Christopher, Ian, Natalie, and my godchildren (official or not): Max, Cristina, Blix, Viggo, Sasha, and Tatum. On the European side of things, I am forever grateful to Yiayia Maria, Akis, Sonia, Donia, Maria, Peter, and Theo Akis. And, as always, thanks and love for my father, Mark.

INDEX